STO

W9-BKR-579

GROWING MONEY

A COMPLETE
(AND COMPLETELY UPDATED!)
INVESTING GUIDE FOR KIDS

Written by Gail Karlitz • Created by Debbie Honig
Illustrated by Stephen Lewis

PSS!
PRICE STERN SLOAN

To Jenny B., who will always be my best investment—G.K.

To my parents, Louis and Mary, who taught me to vary
my investments, and my husband, Stephen, who had the idea
to purchase stocks for kid special occasions and frame the
certificates as artwork, a double investment!—D.H.

ACKNOWLEDGEMENTS

For all of their technical and editing assistance:
Jonathan Brandt, Mac Buhler, David Greene, George Grossman,
Neil Hackman, Larry Leibowitz, Gary Parese, Andrew Vindigni

Special thanks, also, to our "kid" experts:
Jennifer Buhler, Allison Grossman, Matthew Grossman,
Meredith Hackman, Adam Honig

Copyright © 1999, 2001 by Debbie Honig and Gail Karlitz. Illustrations copyright © 1999, 2001 by Stephen
Lewis. All rights reserved. Published by Price Stern Sloan, a imprint of Penguin Putnam Books for Young
Readers, 345 Hudson Street, New York, NY 10014. Printed in the United States of America. Published
simultaneously in Canada. No part of this publication may be reproduced, stored in any retrieval system or
transmitted, in any form or by any means, electronic, mechanical, photocopying, recording, or otherwise,
without the prior written permission of the publisher.

Library of Congress Cataloging-in-Publication Data

Karlitz, Gail.
   Growing money : a complete and completely updated investing guide for kids / written by Gail
Karlitz ; created by Debbie
  Honig ; illustrated by Stephen Lewis.
    p. cm.
   Summary : Explains different types of investing—savings accounts, bonds, stocks, and mutual
funds—and provides information to help make decisions on each kind of investment.
    1. Investments—Juvenile literature. 2. Saving and investment—Juvenile literature. [1. Investments.
2. Saving and investment.] I. Honig, Debbie. II. Lewis, Stephen, ill. III. Title.
  HG4521.K274 1999
  332.6—dc 21   98–54382
                                                CIP

ISBN 0-8431-7702-0   B C D E F G H I J   AC

PSS!
PSS!® is a registered trademark of Penguin Putnam Inc.

TABLE OF CONTENTS

Before You Start

Chapter One
WHERE DO YOU KEEP YOUR MONEY?
1

Chapter Two
WELCOME TO THE WIDE WORLD OF INVESTING
8

Chapter Three
WHAT KIND OF INVESTOR ARE YOU?
13

Chapter Four
THE LOWDOWN ON SAVINGS BANKS
22

Chapter Five
THE ABCs OF BONDS
30

Chapter Six
STOCKS: THE FINANCIAL SUPERMARKETS
42

Chapter Seven
BEHIND THE SCENES
64

Chapter Eight
MAKING MONEY IN THE STOCK MARKET
73

Chapter Nine
READING THE FINANCIAL PAGES
87

Chapter Ten
BUYING AND SELLING STOCKS
96

Chapter Eleven
THE GROWING MONEY INVESTMENT GAME
102

Before You Start

There are many different ways to make money grow. That's what this book is all about. You'll learn about savings accounts, bonds, stocks, and mutual funds, and how to pick the investments that are right for you.

Here are just a few things to keep in mind when you read this book:

$ Because you are a kid, the law refers to you as a "minor." That means that if you want to buy stocks or bonds, your parent or your guardian must be involved. You cannot buy stocks or bonds yourself until you are eighteen.

$ This book tells you about the kinds of things that you should think about when you make money decisions. But do not let any book tell you exactly what to do with your money. You and your parents should always use your own judgment.

$ By the time you read this book, many things will have changed. Every year, companies on the New York Stock Exchange (NYSE) change their names or their symbols. Companies buy other companies, or they sell off parts of themselves. New companies are formed, and some old companies go out of business. There are changes in the economy.

$ Very often in this book we use the names of real companies. That doesn't mean that we are recommending that you invest in them—or not invest in them. We've just used them as examples because they are companies that probably are familiar to you.

We hope you have fun with this book. Most of all, we hope that when you are ready, you will be able to invest wisely as well as successfully.

Chapter One

WHERE DO YOU KEEP YOUR MONEY?

Let's agree on one thing right from the start. If you want to make your money grow, the worst place to keep it is in the pocket of your jeans. You know what happens . . . you either spend it right away or forget to take it out of your pocket. Eventually, your jeans end up on the floor, right there with the rest of the clothes you've worn all week, your schoolbooks, the blanket you kicked off your bed, and other assorted treasures.

What always happens the day

Not a good place for your money!

WHY DO BANKS LOOK LIKE PIGS?

Speaking of piggy banks, why *do* people put money in piggy banks? Does it make sense? Are pigs known for being careful with their money?

The truth is that a long time ago, people had inexpensive pots or jugs in their kitchens that were made of a common clay known as pygg.

When people had some extra money, they would put it into these containers. Eventually, the containers became known as pygg banks, or pyggy banks. Later, someone had a great idea and began to make banks in the shape of pigs.

your room is the messiest? That's right! Your mom makes you clean it, and fast! And what happens to the jeans with the money? You've got it. They end up in the laundry. And then the money is lost and gone forever.

But what about keeping your money in your room—in a safe place, like a piggy bank?

There are a lot of good reasons to keep your money safe in your room. For one thing, it's right there when you need it. You can get to it quickly and easily. Another good thing is that you always know exactly how much money you have. You can take it out at any time and count it.

Of course, the very reason why keeping your money in your room is good can also be the reason why keeping your money in your room is bad. Let's suppose you are saving your money for something big, like a new bike. Your savings are growing nicely. You're up to $35, and then . . . you see a great baseball cap that you really want to buy. It's only $15. And it's so cool!

What a dilemma! You know you shouldn't touch your bike money. But there it is, right in your room, in that piggy bank. It's calling to you, "Come and get me. You know you want to spend me. I'm right here waiting for you. Come get me now, and you'll have that cap today!" Boy, that money sure knows how to be mighty tempting! Money in a piggy bank is money that is easy to spend.

"Come and get me."

Another thing about keeping your money in a piggy bank is that the amount of money you have is never more than what you have put into the piggy bank. If you put in $5 every month, after a year you will have $60. After ten years, you will have $600. No more, no less.

Now, it's always a good idea to save money. So, what's bad about saving money this way? Well, over time, the price of every-thing—from a pack of gum to a new bike—goes up. That means that in ten years, $600 won't buy nearly as much stuff as it will now.

Think about what has happened to the buying power of money. In 1960, a kid with a quarter could buy

$WORD

INFLATION: the general increase in the cost of everything, from cars and houses to burgers and fries

a slice of pizza for 15¢ and a soda for 10¢. Today, you'd probably need at least $2 to buy the same meal! In 1960, a kid who had saved $7 could buy a really great pair of sneakers. Today, you could use that $7 to buy some very cool sneaker laces.

Many adults love to talk about the good old days and how low prices were back then. They sometimes forget that incomes were pretty low then, too. In 1960, the average income per person in this country was $2,219 per year! By 2000, the average income per person was $29,676.

THEN AND NOW

Ask your parents or grandparents about the costs of some things when they were young. Then look at ads in the newspaper for the costs today. Here is a list of some things you can compare.

	THEN	NOW
New car	_____	_____
Sunday newspaper	_____	_____
Dress or shirt	_____	_____
Sneakers	_____	_____
Candy bar	_____	_____
Movie ticket	_____	_____

Some things may have gone down in price.

	THEN	NOW
Calculator	_____	_____
TV	_____	_____
Answering machine	_____	_____

SOMETHING TO THINK ABOUT

Burger King opened its first restaurant in 1954. A burger was 18¢, and a milk shake was 18¢. WHAT DOES THAT MEAL COST TODAY?

THE MOST EXPENSIVE MOVIES EVER MADE

As of 1939, *Gone with the Wind* . . . . $4.25 million

As of 1960, *Spartacus* . . . . $12 million

As of 1997, *Titanic* . . . . $200 million

Aside from the fact that a specific amount of money loses some of its buying power as time goes by, there's one more reason why people usually don't keep their money at home. If you have a lot of money (which would be a really nice problem to have), it gets a little hard to find places for it all. A million dollars in dollar bills . . .

$ laid end to end, would run for 97 miles.

$ stacked on top of one another would be 358 feet high—as high as a thirty-five-story skyscraper.

$ would weigh more than a ton—2,041 pounds, to be exact.

Of course, no one would really keep a million dollar bills around. They would at least trade them in for ten thousand hundred-dollar bills!

J. PAUL GETTY,
who was one of the richest men in America,
once said, "If you can actually count your
money, then you are not really a rich man."

Our government does print money in higher denominations than hundred-dollar bills, but those bills are not used by the general public. Each year, more money is printed for the board game Monopoly than for the entire United States Treasury.

HOW LONG DOES MONEY LAST?

The Bureau of Engraving and Printing produces additional paper money to replace money that is damaged, destroyed, lost, or just plain worn out. Denominations that are used more frequently have shorter life spans than those that are not used very often.

DENOMINATION	AVERAGE LIFE SPAN
$1 bill	18 months
$5 bill	15 months
$10 bill	18 months
$20 bill	2 years
$50 bill	5 years
$100 bill	8½ years
Coins	About 25 years

TRIVIA FACT
It costs 2.6 cents to print each bill!

WHO'S WHO ON OUR MONEY

$1 ....George Washington (first U.S. president)

$2.............Thomas Jefferson (third U.S. president)

$5.............Abraham Lincoln (sixteenth U.S. president)

$10...........Alexander Hamilton (first U.S. treasury secretary)

$20 ....Andrew Jackson (seventh U.S. president)

$50 ....Ulysses S. Grant (eighteenth U.S. president)

$100 ....Benjamin Franklin

$500 ....(not printed since 1946) William McKinley (twenty-fifth U.S. president)

$1,000 ....(not printed since 1946) Grover Cleveland (twenty-second and twenty-fourth U.S. president)

$5,000.......(not printed since 1946) James Madison (fourth U.S. president)

$10,000......(not printed since 1946) Salmon P. Chase (twenty-fifth U.S. treasury secretary)

$100,000 ....(only printed from 12/34 to 1/35) Woodrow Wilson (twenty-eighth U.S. president)

YOU CAN MAKE MONEY WITH YOUR MONEY

It just doesn't make sense to keep your money at home. You're tempted to spend it, and the prices of the things you want keep going up. The longer you hold on to your money, the less it's worth. And, if you did save a fortune, you'd break your back trying to lift it all!

Wait! Don't rush out to spend all your money right now!

There are many ways you can save your money so that the amount you put in actually grows, even if you don't add a cent more. When you do that, you are making your money earn more money for you. You are an investor.

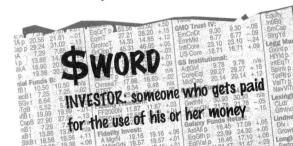

$WORD

INVESTOR: someone who gets paid for the use of his or her money

Chapter Two

WELCOME TO THE WIDE WORLD OF INVESTING

All investors hope to get paid for letting other people use their money for a while. Banks, companies, cities, and even countries all need to go to investors—lots of investors—to get the money they need.

THE MOST COMMON INVESTMENT CHOICES

There are many ways to invest money. The most common ways are in savings accounts at banks, in bonds, in stocks, and in mutual funds.

Banks pay you for keeping your money in a savings account. The bank uses your money while it's in the account. If you want to take out some or all of your money, you may do that at any time. You may also deposit more money into your account at any time.

After you open a savings account, you will get bank statements in the mail to keep track of how much money is in your account. Some banks send statements every month; others

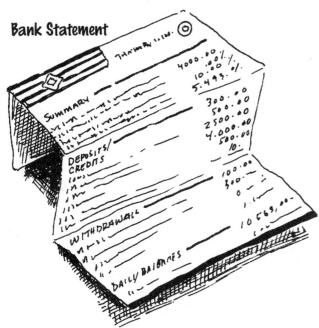

Bank Statement

send them every quarter (every three months). Many banks also allow you to view your account information on line at their Web sites.

When you look at your statement, you can see a record of every deposit and every withdrawal you made. You will also see extra money that the bank has deposited into your account. That extra money is called interest. The bank is paying you that extra money because you are letting them use the money in your account.

Bonds are loans to companies or governments. The company or government that borrows your money promises to pay you back by a specific date and also to pay you interest for the use of your money.

When you invest in a bond, you may get a bond certificate. The bond certificate spells out the details of the bond: how much money has been borrowed, how much interest you will be paid for the use of your money, and the deadline for paying you back.

Many people give U.S. Savings Bonds as gifts to newborn babies or as birthday presents to kids. By buying these savings bonds, people are lending money to our country to help it continue to grow.

Stocks are small pieces (or shares) of companies. People who own stock in a company are called shareholders. When you are a shareholder, the company may share some of its profits with you . . . if the company has profits.

When you buy stock in a company, you are not lending money to the company. Companies do not promise to pay back money that they get when you buy shares of their stock. If you do want your money back, you may try to sell your stock to someone else. When you sell your stock, the price of the stock may be much higher than it was when you bought it. If that happens, you will make a lot of money on the sale. But the price of the stock also can be lower than it was when you bought it. If that happens, you will lose money if you sell it.

Mutual funds are collections of lots of different stocks or bonds. A fund manager chooses a group of stocks (or bonds) for the collection. When you buy shares in a mutual fund, you and many other people each own a portion of this whole collection, but you don't own any specific stock or bond. With mutual funds, as with individual stocks, you can make or lose money.

The four most common investments (in bank accounts, bonds, stocks, and mutual funds) are different from one another in several ways.

ARE ALL INVESTMENTS RISKY?

Some investments are very risky. When you put money into a high-risk investment, like buying stock in a brand-new company, your money may grow a lot. Or you may lose it all.

Some investments, like savings accounts or U.S. Savings

3 1833 03859 1555

Bonds, involve almost no risk. You know exactly how much your money will grow, and you will not lose any of the money you invest.

Investments differ also in how quickly or slowly your money grows. Some investments are good for people who can wait a long time for their money to grow. Other investments are good for people who want to be able to take out their money whenever they need it.

So, where should you invest your money? Have you heard the story about the girl who was taking eggs from her family's farm to market? She was going to sell them so that the family could have money for food and clothes. On her way to the market, the handle on her basket broke. When the basket landed on the ground, all the eggs cracked. The girl's family got no money, and she learned a lesson: Never put all your eggs in one basket.

Most financial experts agree with that motto. They usually advise each person to have several different kinds of investments. How much of your money you put in each type of investment will be up to you. It all depends on how much risk you want to take and how long you plan to leave your money invested.

Have you ever heard of a baseball or basketball team that won every game in the season? Probably not!

$WORD PORTFOLIO: the collection of all your investments

It's the same with investing. You can't win them all. No matter how hard you try, you won't pick a winner every time. When you diversify (make different kinds of investments) there is a good chance that some of your investments will make money, even if others don't. You will have less risk of losing all your money.

Investing can be lots of fun. You should invest in the kinds of things that interest you. If seeing your investment go up and down in value very often will make you nervous, you might want to put only a little money into high-risk investments. If you think you will be bored with investments that are predictable, then you should put more of your money in high-risk investments.

Chapter Three

WHAT KIND OF INVESTOR ARE YOU?

Right now, you are not old enough to make actual investments on your own. Even if you have money in the bank, you still need a parent to do your investing for you. But it's never too early to learn about investments or what kind of investor you want to be.

There are all kinds of investors, just as there are all kinds of people. Some people enjoy taking chances. They are like the people who are eager to try bungee jumping. They are risk lovers. Others want to be safe and sure. They are like the people who won't go outside in a thunderstorm because of the small chance of being hit by a bolt of lightening. Those people are risk avoiders. Most people are somewhere in the middle.

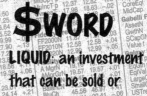

$WORD

LIQUID: an investment that can be sold or converted back into cash very quickly and easily

RISK FACTORS

Odds of being struck
by lightning in your lifetime . . . . .1 in 9,000

Odds of dying
on a fifty-mile drive . . . . .1 in 1,000,000

Odds of winning
a lottery .1 in 7,000,000

KNOW YOURSELF

Take this short quiz to find out what kind of investor you are. Don't be nervous—the quiz is fun. There are no right or wrong answers, and you can't pass or fail. It's important to be honest with yourself—don't pretend to be somebody else. (You might want to have your parents or friends take the same quiz. See whether their attitudes about money are the same as yours.)

WHO ARE YOU?

1. **You are offered a chance to be part of the first colony on the moon. You:**

   a) ask how soon the flight leaves and go home to pack

   b) agree to be part of the setup team . . . *if* you can come home after six months

   c) stay on Earth and enjoy breathing without an oxygen tank

2. **Last month, you went to a new restaurant. Since then, you haven't stopped thinking about how great your meal was. You go back this month, and the waiter recommends the special of the day: alligator tail with artichoke sauce. You:**

   a) order the same wonderful meal you had last time

   b) go for the special of the day

   c) convince your friend to order the special, so you can try it

3. **In the music store, you see a new CD. You never heard of the group, but the sign over the display says they're the hottest band of the century (and the lead singer is adorable!). You:**

   a) buy it so you can be the first in your school to discover a new sound

   b) ask the manager if there's a demo you can listen to

   c) look for something by a group that you know you like

15¢

4. You're on a TV game show, and you have just won $3,000 to decorate your room any way you want. Now you have to decide to keep the money or trade it for the secret prize. The secret prize may be a rubber chicken, or it may be a check for a million dollars! You:

    a) go for the secret prize—if you don't get the million dollars, you can work on a comedy routine with the rubber chicken

    b) keep the money and plan your new room

    c) do whatever most of the audience votes for you to do

5. You and your friends are at the brand-new town pool. There is a *very* high diving board that hasn't been tried out yet. You:

    a) stick to the low diving board, showing off the cannonball skills you perfected last summer

    b) rush to be the first in line to try out the high board

    c) wait until a few of your friends use it and see what they think

6. It's the very end of the fourth quarter of the big basketball game. Your team is two points down, and you have the ball. You:

    a) pass it to Slam Dunk Sammy, who most likely will make two points to tie the game

    b) pass it to Long Shot Louie, who might make three points to win

    c) pass it to Captain Carl and let him decide who should get it

7. Your mom won a sales contest at work. The prize is a family trip to Big Kahuna Island in the South Pacific. Big Kahuna is a tropical paradise, but it has a huge volcano right in the middle of it. There's a one-in-five hundred chance that the volcano will erupt sometime this year. You:

    a) agree to go to the island but make your parents promise you will stay as far from the volcano as possible

    b) plead with your mother to give the trip to someone else

    c) get ready to go and hope that your family will agree to camp out on the most beautiful spot on the island—the top of the huge volcano

8. You pass Hometown Gifts and see that they just got a shipment of the newest limited-edition Beanie Beauties. They're selling for $50 each, with a limit of two per customer. Regular Beanie Beauties are selling for $6 each. You:

    a) borrow $100 from your parents, because you believe they will be worth $1,000 each someday soon

    b) spend $12 on two of the regular ones, which may or may not be worth more than that someday

    c) pass up the Beanie Beauties and buy a CD that you know you'll enjoy

9. You go to the multiplex with your friend to catch the new horror movie you've both been dying to see for weeks. Unfortunately, you mixed up the show times and you arrive an hour late. You:

a) go to a movie your friend insists she's heard is good, even though it looks weird and boring to you

b) spot a cool-looking poster for a new movie that neither of you has heard of but decide to go anyway

c) buy tickets for the movie you and your friend saw a couple of weeks ago—it wasn't that great, but you could sit through it again

10. It's almost time for grades to be in, and your teacher asks you to stay after class. At this point, your math grade averages out to a C+. Your teacher gives you the following options. Which will you choose? You:

a) can take a pop quiz on the spot, and, if you do well, you can bring your grade up to a B+, but if you do poorly, your grade could fall to a C-

b) can agree to take home some extra-credit work that can't hurt your grade but could bring it up to only a B-

c) can retake one of the tests you bombed, which could bring your grade up to a B or down to a C

NOW, SEE HOW MANY POINTS YOU GET FOR EACH ANSWER.

1.	a = 5	b = 2	c = 1	6.	a = 1	b = 5	c = 2
2.	a = 1	b = 5	c = 2	7.	a = 2	b = 1	c = 5
3.	a = 5	b = 2	c = 1	8.	a = 5	b = 2	c = 1
4.	a = 5	b = 1	c = 2	9.	a = 2	b = 5	c = 1
5.	a = 1	b = 5	c = 2	10.	a = 5	b = 1	c = 2

YOUR TOTAL SCORE _____

38–50 points Risk Lover: Taking a chance is exciting. Whether your decision turns out to be right or wrong is not that important to you. The result may be great or awful, but the chance of its being great is worth it. Risk lovers are often referred to as aggressive investors.

20–37 points Moderate Risk Taker: You enjoy taking a chance, but you try to find out as much as you can first. You are comfortable with a little risk, but not too much. People like you are often known as moderate investors.

10–19 points Risk Avoider: You like to know what is going to happen. Taking a chance makes you feel nervous and uncomfortable. You want to be as sure as you can that you don't make any huge mistakes. People who are uncomfortable with a lot of risk are known as conservative investors.

You are a

☐ Risk lover

☐ Moderate risk taker

☐ Risk avoider

19¢

INVESTING FOR YOUR PERSONALITY

Now that you know a little bit about your investing personality, you can start to explore some of the different ways to invest and see which one suits you best.

As you learn about each type of investing, you should think about these questions:

$ Could I end up with less money than I started with?

$ How quickly can I get my money back?

$ Does this investment match my investing personality?

$ How can I check out what I need to know about this investment?

There are some investments that have very little risk, where you know that almost certainly you will not lose the money you start with. With low-risk investments, you will earn some more money, and you usually know how much. Lending money to the United States government is a good example of a low-risk investment. You can be sure that our government will be in business for a long time and that it will pay its debts. That investment is very safe, but you will earn only a small amount on it.

How can you invest in the United States? One way is to buy U.S. Savings Bonds. When you read the chapter about bonds, you will learn about treasury bonds, notes, and bills, which are other things you can invest in to lend money to our country.

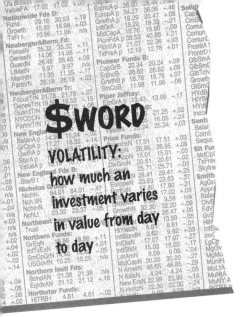

$WORD

VOLATILITY: how much an investment varies in value from day to day

HOW QUICKLY CAN I GET MY MONEY BACK?

When you keep your money in your room, you can get to it very quickly. Some investments are like that also. You can take your money out whenever you want. Most accounts at savings banks are very liquid—you can withdraw as much of your money as you want, whenever you want. There is also a special kind of savings account, called a CD (certificate of deposit), that pays a higher rate of interest if you agree that you will not take your money out of the account for a certain amount of time (that can be anywhere from thirty days to ten years or more).

There are investments (some stocks, for example) whose value goes up and down a lot. That becomes a problem if the investment is at a very low point just when you need your money. When you know that you won't need your money for a long time, a low point is not as much of a problem. If you are in fifth grade now and you are saving for college, you have the time to wait until your investment goes up again.

Chapter Four

THE LOWDOWN ON SAVINGS BANKS

Savings banks keep your money safe for you. You are very unlikely to lose your money, and spending it all right away is hard, since you have to go to the bank or an automatic teller machine (ATM) to withdraw it.

Savings banks are unlike piggy banks in two important ways. First of all, savings banks pay you for keeping your money there. Second, the money that you deposit in a savings account is not really in the bank building where you make your deposit. In fact, banks usually don't keep huge amounts of cash in their buildings. Banks use your deposits to earn more money for themselves.

WILLIE SUTTON,
a famous outlaw, was once asked, "Willie, why do you keep robbing banks?" Willie replied, "Because that's where the money is."

Banks do keep some money that people have deposited, but most of the money is invested in different ways so the bank can earn more money. Banks lend money to customers who want to buy homes or cars, send their children to college, or even start new businesses.

$ QUESTION: The government tells banks how much of their total deposits they have to keep in their buildings. Usually it is about:
a) 10%
b) 50%
c) 90%

Answer: (a) 10%

What if you want to take your money out of the bank? Not to worry. There is always enough money right at the bank for you to take out all your money.

What if everyone wants to take out all their money on the same day? You don't have to worry about that either. Our government guarantees your deposits are safe. The Federal Deposit Insurance Corporation (FDIC) will lend the bank enough money to pay each depositor up to $100,000 even if the bank itself runs out of money. If you have more than $100,000 (lucky you!), just put it in more than one bank. The FDIC will insure up to $100,000 in each bank where you have an account.

How much money the bank pays you depends on the interest rate. The interest rate is the amount the bank will pay you for every dollar you keep in your account. If the interest rate is 5 percent, the bank will pay you 5¢ a year for every

$ TIP: Do not deposit valuable coins (rare old ones) in your savings account! They will not be there when you try to get them back. You may want to put them in a safe-deposit box at a bank. That is like a super-secure piggy bank. Besides valuable coin collections, or special coins or dollars with a person's birth year on them, jewelry or important papers also can be stored in safe-deposit boxes.

dollar in your account. If you have $100 in your account, they pay you $5 a year. For $1,000, they will pay you $50 a year.

Your money keeps growing this way. The bank pays you interest on the money you deposit. If you leave that interest in your account, the bank will pay you interest on that money also. That is called compound interest!

Say your parents put $1,000 in a savings account for you. If the interest rate is 5 percent, at the end of the first year, your account will have about $1,050 in it—your original $1,000 plus an extra 5 percent, or $50.

If you leave your money there for another year, your account will have about $1,102.50 in it. In the second year, you earn $50 interest on your original deposit, *plus* another $2.50 interest on the interest you earned in the first year.

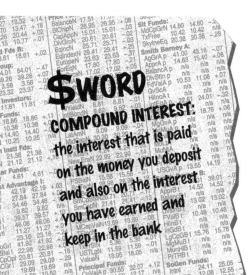

$WORD

COMPOUND INTEREST: the interest that is paid on the money you deposit and also on the interest you have earned and keep in the bank

If the interest rate were 5 percent, after five years your bank account would earn a total of $276.

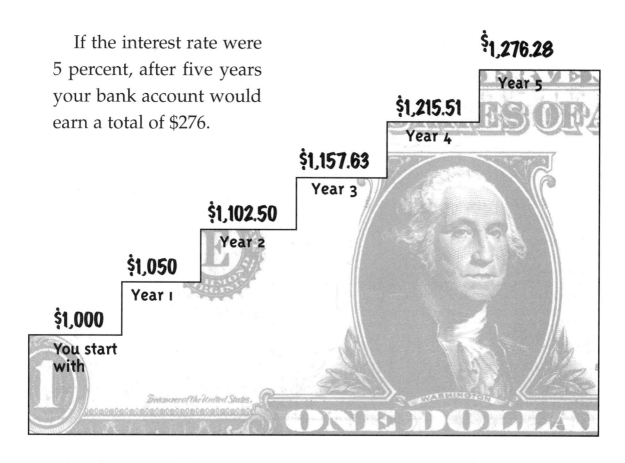

$1,276.28
Year 5

$1,215.51
Year 4

$1,157.63
Year 3

$1,102.50
Year 2

$1,050
Year 1

$1,000
You start with

DOUBLE YOUR MONEY

Here's a neat formula to figure out how long it will take you to double your money in a savings account.

72 divided by interest rates = number of years to double your money

What does that mean?

If you deposit $100 and get 6 percent interest, in twelve years you will double your money. You will have $200!

12 YEARS LATER

That's because 72 divided by the interest rate (6) equals 12. If you deposit $100 and you get only 5 percent interest, it will take almost fourteen and a half years to double your money (72 divided by 5 = 14.4).

$ QUESTION: How long would it take to double your money if you get 8 percent interest?

Answer: 9 years (72/8=9)

As you can imagine, it takes a long time for money to double at the interest rates that savings banks usually pay. If you have $100 and your savings bank is paying 6 percent interest, you should think about whether it is worth waiting twelve years to have $200. Twelve years from now, will $200 buy more than $100 does right now?

HOW DO BANKS MAKE MONEY?

Banks would quickly go out of business if all they did was take deposits and pay interest on them. Banks need to make money to pay for their buildings, employees, telephones, electricity, and other services. Banks are also in business to make a profit.

Banks make money by combining the money from all their depositors and lending that money to other people or companies. The customers of

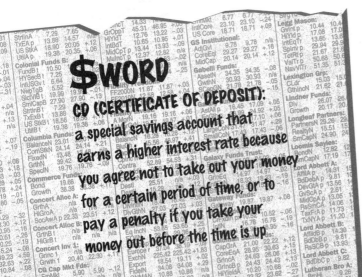

$WORD

CD (CERTIFICATE OF DEPOSIT): a special savings account that earns a higher interest rate because you agree not to take out your money for a certain period of time, or to pay a penalty if you take your money out before the time is up.

the bank who borrow the money are people who may want to buy cars or houses or go to college, and local businesses who may want to expand. When the banks lend money, they charge interest on the loans.

HOW A BANK MAKES MONEY

Congratulations! You are the first person to call the radio station with the word of the day, and you win $5,000! You decide to put the money in the bank to save for college. The bank pays 5 percent interest on all deposits. At the end of one year, you will have $5,250 in your account (your original $5,000 plus $250 interest).

The same day that you win the radio contest, Cousin Justin goes to the same bank and borrows $5,000 for one year to help him buy a new car. The bank is charging 9 percent interest on loans. At the end of the year, Cousin Justin has to pay the bank $5,450.

The bank earned $450 in interest from Cousin Justin. It paid you $250 in interest on your deposit. The bank earned a profit of $200.

If you were to borrow $1,000 from a bank for one year, at an annual interest rate of 9 percent, at the end of the year you would have to pay back the original $1,000 plus 9 percent interest ($90). The total you would repay would be $1,090. The interest rate charged for loans is always higher than the interest rate the paid for deposits.

You saw that when you deposit money in a savings account, the bank keeps paying you interest. When you borrow money from a bank, you keep paying interest until the loan is paid. This interest can add up to a lot of money.

PUTTING YOUR MONEY IN A SAVINGS BANK

$ Before you select a savings bank, compare the interest rates of all the banks in your neighborhood. Interest rates change often, but you will want to start with the highest rate you can.

$ Find out if you can get a higher rate of interest if you keep your money in a certificate of deposit (CD). Banks offer different choices of CDs with different rates of interest for different lengths of time. Consider what choice is best for you.

$ You should also think about whether the bank is convenient for you and your parents and whether you can mail in your deposits.

$ Some banks charge you a monthly fee if you keep less than a certain amount of money in your account. Be sure to ask about that before you open your account.

You need to have a parent with you to open a savings bank account. You and your parent can open the account by going into the nearest branch of the bank you select.

You can always look at your bank statement to see how much money is in your account and how much interest you have earned. Some banks also allow you to receive that information over the phone or on line. You can also find out your balance through your bank's ATM.

WHO SHOULD PUT MONEY IN A SAVINGS ACCOUNT?

The good things about savings accounts are that they are very safe and you can get your money easily if you need it.

Remember, you should never put all your eggs in one basket. Risk lovers should put some money in a savings bank, especially if they are going to need some of the money soon. If you are saving money to buy holiday presents for friends or family, a savings bank is a good choice. Risk avoiders may want to put a bigger portion of their money in a savings bank but also may want to put *some* money in other, higher-risk investments, which may pay more.

Chapter Five

THE ABCs OF BONDS

Have you ever heard of Idealtown, USA? (If you have, write to us right away, because we thought we made it up just for this book.)

Anyway, Idealtown is the perfect place to live. The weather is great all year. There has never been a snowstorm, a hurricane, a flood, or an earthquake. The houses are nice and cozy, the streets are clean and safe; the schools are great; the stores are beautiful; and the neighbors are as friendly as can be.

Idealtown was a nice, well-kept secret for many years. Then, in 2001, some people from a big, famous magazine came to take pictures and write stories, and before anyone knew what happened, about two thousand new families decided to move to Idealtown.

The friendly Idealtown people were happy to have all these new neighbors. There were just a few small problems. With all those

$WORD

TERM: the amount of time from the date the bond is issued until it matures

new families coming to Idealtown, they needed to build new schools, hire new teachers, expand the library and hospital, and maybe even build more playgrounds and soccer fields. Where would they get the money?

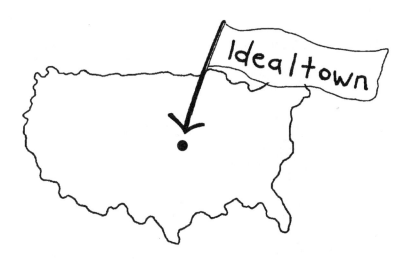

The town needed $100 million to pay for everything they wanted to do. They decided to borrow the money from investors by issuing bonds. To borrow $100 million, Idealtown issued twenty thousand bonds for $5,000 each, with an interest rate of 6 percent and a term of twenty years. When Idealtown had to pay back the money it borrowed (in 2021), the bond-holders would get all their money back ($5,000 for each bond they bought). During the twenty years that they held the bonds, the bondholders would receive 6 percent interest a year, or $300 for each bond they owned.

When you invest in a bond, you may get a piece of paper that describes the details of the borrower's promises. When a person writes out a promise to pay back a loan, it is often called an IOU (a short way of saying "I Owe You"). The IOU from a city government, like Idealtown, is called a bond certificate.

April 1, 2002

I, **Betty Borrower**, do hereby promise that I will repay **Suzie Saver** $25 on June 1, 2002.

Because Suzie is my best friend, she is not charging me any interest.

Betty Borrower
Signature of Borrower

Suzie Saver
Signature of Lender

A bond certificate is just like an IOU. It tells you important things about the bond.

- **$ Face value or par:** the amount of money you will be paid back if you hold the bond until its maturity date
- **$ Maturity date:** the latest date by which the borrower must repay the loan
- **$ Coupon rate or yield:** the interest rate that the borrower is paying, based on the face value of the bond
- **$ Coupon payments:** how much will be paid at every interest period

The bond expires on the maturity date. That is the date the loan must be repaid to you, the investor. The amount of time from the day the bond is issued to the day it expires is called the term of the bond. The term may be as long as thirty years (or more), but an investor can buy or sell the bonds at any time

Bond...
Growth 38.38 36.38 +.17
Concert Alloc A:
GrthA n/a n/a n/a
HiGroA n/a n/a n/a
SocAwA p 22.33 23.51 +.12
Concert Alloc B:
GrthB t n/a n/a n/a
HiGrB t n/a n/a n/a

$WORDS

MATURITY DATE: the latest date that the money borrowed for the bond can be repaid

EXPIRE: what happens when a bond reaches its maturity date. (It doesn't mean the bond has died!)

ISSUE: to create and sell stocks or bonds

during the term. Before the maturity date, the value of the bond may be more or less than the full, or face, value. The investor who owns the bond at the maturity date receives the face value for it.

KINDS OF BONDS

Corporate bonds are issued by companies. They can be for any term. They usually have a higher interest rate than government bonds, but they are also riskier investments. Corporate bonds are usually issued in multiples of $1,000 or $5,000. Investors usually receive the interest on corporate bonds every six months.

Municipal bonds are issued by state and local governments. Municipal bonds are usually issued in multiples of $5,000, and interest payments are made every six months. Municipal bonds usually pay lower interest rates than corporate bonds. So, why would anyone want to buy them? It's a little complicated to understand because it has to do with taxes, and you don't have to pay taxes right now. When you're older, you'll learn that people have to pay taxes on the interest their money earns. That means they have to give the government some of that money. There is an exception for the interest earned from municipal bonds—there is no federal income tax on that interest. So, people are willing to earn less interest on municipal bonds, since they get to keep more of that interest.

Treasuries are bonds issued by the United States government.

People often say that treasuries are the safest investments because they are backed by the "full faith and credit" of our government. That means that it is very, very unlikely that our government would not be able to pay back its loans.

The United States government borrows money by issuing:

$ Savings bonds, which can be bought for as little as $25

$ Treasury bills, which have a maturity of less than a year (usually three months or six months). The minimum purchase of a treasury bill is $1,000.

$ Treasury notes, which mature in one to ten years. The minimum purchase is $1,000, and you can buy them in multiples of $1,000.

$ Treasury bonds, which have a maturity of ten to thirty or forty years. They also have a minimum purchase of $1,000, and you can buy them in multiples of $1,000.

You can buy Treasury notes or Treasury bonds at face value, just as you would corporate or municipal bonds. You get interest every six months, and at the end of the term you get your original money back.

Treasury bills (and some U.S. Savings Bonds) work differently. You buy the bond at a discount, which means that you pay less than face value. So, for a $10,000 U.S. Savings Bond, you might pay only $9,700. You do not receive interest every six months. But when you turn in the bond at its maturity date, you receive the $10,000 face value of the bond. So you've made $300. This "extra" $300 is really your interest. In this case, the total yield percent would be 3.1 percent.

$300 divided by $9,700=3.1 percent

A VERY LONG-TERM INVESTMENT

In 1993, the Disney Corporation issued corporate bonds with a term of one hundred years. They mature in 2093!

THE FIRST U.S. BONDS

The first major bond issue in the United States was in 1790, when the government issued $80 million in bonds to help pay for the Revolutionary War debt.

THE NEWS ON U.S. SAVINGS BONDS

Traditional, EE Series U.S. Savings Bonds are bought at half of their face value and redeemed at face value when they mature. The term of the bond, or number of years for the bond to mature, depends on the year in which it was purchased.

Another type of U.S. Savings Bond, the I Series, is purchased at full face value, and interest is added to that amount. When you buy the bond, there is a fixed interest rate that is guaranteed for thirty years. Then there is additional interest calculated every six months, based on the rate of inflation.

For more information about savings bonds, go to www.savingsbonds.gov.

$ FACTS

Over fifty-five million people own U.S. Savings Bonds. By the end of 2000, Americans were purchasing about $10 million in bonds each month through the Internet alone.

WASHINGTON

HOW SAFE IS A BOND?

As far as investments go, most bonds are a good, safe bet. When you buy a bond, you know how much interest you will get. There is also a very, very good chance that you will get all your money back if you keep the bond until its maturity date. Still, there are cases when the issuer (the government or company that borrowed your money) has business or financial problems and does not have the money to pay interest to the bondholders. When that happens, the borrower defaults. Every once in a while, the borrower does not have the money to pay back the original loan when it is due. Then the investor loses his or her original investment as well.

"You can trust me!"

United States government bonds are very safe. They are just about 100 percent guaranteed against default.

Municipal bonds are a little more risky. Although it is very rare, there have been times when a local government has not had enough money to pay the interest owed to the investors. Even when that has happened, the local government has almost always been able to fix its financial problems in time to pay back the money due on the maturity date of the municipal bond.

Corporate bonds can be safe or risky. If the company is very successful and looks as though it will continue to be successful, there is almost no risk. The more financial problems the company is having, the greater the risk that it may not be able to pay back the money it borrows.

WHO SHOULD BUY BONDS?

People who are more risk avoiders than risk lovers usually invest a lot of their money in bonds. They know just how much money they will get from the interest payments, how much the bond will be worth at maturity, and how long it will be until the bond matures.

Does that mean that bonds should be the only place to invest your money? No way. Can you guess why?

Besides the risk of default, another thing to think about when investing in bonds is inflation. When the bond matures, you get back all the money you paid for it. But that money may not be worth as much as when you bought the bond—even with all the interest money you received over the years.

Suppose you invest $10,000 in a thirty-year bond that pays 6 percent interest. That means that you will get $600 every year for thirty years, for a total of $18,000. You will also get your $10,000 back, so you will have received $28,000 in total.

"I'd like to buy this new paperback book for $789."

In the year 3002

Sounds pretty good, right? But remember, nobody knows what things will cost in the future. In 2002, you may be able to buy more stuff with $10,000 than you will be able to buy with $28,000 in 2032. So, is getting the same $600 a year every year for thirty years a good investment? No one can really answer that now!

If you hold your $10,000 bond until maturity, you will almost certainly get your $10,000 back. But suppose you don't want to wait until then. You can sell your bond to someone else, but you may not get as much money as you paid for it.

When you get $600 interest for your investment of $10,000, you are getting a return of 6 percent. What if the banks begin to offer higher interest rates before your thirty-year bond matures? Say the banks begin to offer 8 percent interest ten years after you buy your thirty-year bond. If you put your $10,000 in the bank then, you would earn $800 a year instead of only $600. Should you sell your bond and put the money in a bank? You can, but who would want to buy your bond? No one would want to get 6 percent interest with a bond when he or she could get 8 percent from the bank.

The biggest influence on the price at which you can sell your bond is the interest rate that other investments are paying. If people can get higher interest rates in other ways that are just as safe, no one will want to buy your bond. And so the value of your bond will go down. Let's see how that works.

If someone were to buy your bond, he or she would want to get an 8 percent return on the investment, since that is what could be earned in a bank. Your $10,000 bond will pay the new owner $600 a year. How can the new owner make sure that he or she gets an 8 percent return?

Well, let's say he or she offers only $7,500 for the $10,000 bond. He or she will still get $600 a year in interest. That doesn't change. Six hundred dollars is 6 percent of $10,000, but it comes out to 8 percent of $7,500. Do the math and you'll see:

$$\$7{,}500 \text{ times } .08 = \$600$$

When the bond reaches maturity, the new owner will be repaid the original $10,000 from the company that issued the bond.

So, if you really needed the money you invested, you could sell your bond. But would you want to sell it for $2,500 less than you paid for it? It's important for you to remember that risk when you buy bonds that do not mature for a long time.

HOW DO YOU KNOW HOW RISKY A BOND IS?

Fortunately, it's easy to find out a bond's riskiness. There are bond-rating services that do lots of research into all companies and governments that issue bonds. They give a rating to each bond. The rating indicates how likely it is that the borrower will not be able to pay back its loans. The higher the rating, the more likely the loans will be repaid. A rating of AAA is better than a rating of BBB.

Bonds with the lowest rating (CCC) are often called junk bonds. They are usually issued by companies that are facing a lot of financial problems. Sometimes these companies are able to hire new management, solve their problems, and pay back their loans. Sometimes they are not. Because these companies are very risky, they usually have to pay very high interest rates in order to get people to buy their bonds.

DO YOUR HOMEWORK

Before you buy a bond, be sure you check the bond's rating to get an idea of how safe the financial experts think that investment is. You can find out how a bond is rated by looking at the reports in the library or on the Internet, or by calling your broker (if your family has one).

Two of the biggest and best-known bond-rating services are Moody's and Standard & Poor's. Here is how they rate bonds.

	Moody's	S&P
Super safe	Aaa	AAA
Really, really, safe	Aa1	AA+
	Aa2	AA
	Aa3	AA-
Really safe	A1	A+
	A2	A
	A3	A-
Not very safe	Baa1	BBB+
	Baa2	BBB
	Baa3	BBB-
Pretty risky	Ba1	BB+
	Ba2	BB
	Ba3	BB-
Lots of risk	B1	B+
	B2	B
	B3	B-
Very, very risky	Caa	CCC+
	—	CCC
	—	CCC-
	Ca	—
Is, or may be, in default	C	—
	—	D

BUYING BONDS

Almost all local banks have applications for buying U.S. Savings Bonds. When you return the completed application with the money you want to invest, the bank forwards it to a Federal Reserve Bank, which issues the savings bond and mails it to you. You can also purchase U.S. Savings Bonds on line with a major credit card. And, to make it even easier for U.S. citizens to buy these bonds, the government has created

EasySaver—a way to have money automatically taken out of your bank account each month to purchase bonds. Other types of bonds (corporate and municipal) must be purchased through an investment salesperson or a financial advisor.

CHECKING ON YOUR BONDS

Some newspapers do list prices for a few bonds that have been bought and sold in the past week. The *New York Times* publishes this list on Saturdays, and the *Wall Street Journal* publishes it on Mondays. But most bonds are not listed here. The best way to check on the value of a bond is to look in the library or on the Internet, or ask a broker.

SOME LAST WORDS ON BONDS

Even risk lovers sometimes buy bonds. If you know you will need your money soon, you may want to buy some low-risk, short-term bonds. You may not make as much money as you would with some other investments, but at least there is an excellent chance that you will get back all your money when you need it. And always remember that it is a good policy to diversify. Even the most daredevil investors usually own some bonds.

Chapter Six

STOCKS: THE FINANCIAL SUPERMARKETS

You may not have noticed, but almost every newscast on TV or radio mentions something about the stock market. All day there are news reports about whether the stock market is up or down, if trading is heavy or light, and where the market closed for the day.

Why do the newspeople think it's so important to give us this information all day? For one thing, the stock market is a very important force in your life. You probably didn't realize this, but the stock market can affect what products are available for you to buy; how expensive the things we want will be, and even whether there will be jobs in the fields you want to work in when you graduate from school. The second reason stock-market news is important to so many people is that almost half of the families in America have money invested in the stock market. Even cities, colleges, and banks

$WORD

STOCK MARKET: not a place, but the business of buying and selling stocks.

invest in the stock market. Whether the stock market goes up or down may influence how soon your parents can retire, whether they can afford to send you to college, how much the college you want to attend can afford to grow, and many other things.

So, if you want to try to make your money make a lot more money for you, you need to know what the stock market is and how it works. The stock market is in the news so often that you may already know more than you realize. Let's begin with this short quiz. (The answers are at the end of the quiz, but try not to peek.)

GROWING MONEY
Stock Market Savvy Quiz

Circle one answer for each question.

1. Wall Street is:

  a) an expression that includes all buying and selling of stock

  b) a place where you have to go to buy stocks

  c) a wall where a large billboard shows the price of every stock

  d) all of the above

2. You can find a stock exchange in:

  a) Tokyo

  b) New York

  c) Chicago

  d) all of the above

3. When you buy stock in a company, you are usually entitled to:

    a) vote on some of the decisions being made by the company

    b) buy all its products at half price

    c) get a summer job at company headquarters

    d) all of the above

4. In order to buy stock, you must:

    a) go to Wall Street in New York City

    b) own a computer and get on the Internet

    c) be able to invest at least $20,000

    d) be older than eighteen or have your parents invest for you

5. When people talk about how much risk there is in buying a stock, they mean:

    a) whether the company produces products that may be dangerous

    b) how likely it is that you may lose some of the money you invest

    c) whether the president of the company likes to go skydiving

    d) all of the above

6. A broker is:

    a) anyone who has less money than you do

    b) a person who does the actual buying and selling of stock for people

    c) someone who decides on the price for a stock

    d) all of the above

7. The price of a stock is determined by:
   a) a vote by all the shareholders of the stock
   b) the U.S. secretary of the Treasury
   c) the people who want to buy and sell it
   d) the president of the company

8. To get information about a company's financial history and outlook for the future, you need to:
   a) know someone who works there
   b) read the *Wall Street Journal* every Monday
   c) read the public reports the company has written
   d) call a private detective because this information is not available to the public

9. When you select a stock to buy, it is very important to:
   a) be sure you like the letters it uses for its symbol in the newspaper
   b) ask everyone you meet if he or she has any "hot tips"
   c) look only at stocks that have very low prices
   d) learn all you can about the company, its products, and its past performance

10. The company's published reports may tell you:
   a) if they are being sued by anyone
   b) their sales and costs for the past five years
   c) the names of everyone on the board of directors
   d) all of the above

11. When you buy stock in a company, you are called a:
   a) director

b) lender
c) creditor
d) shareholder

12. **If the price of a stock went up last year, this year it will:**
    a) increase again
    b) go back down to its original price
    c) stay the same for a year
    d) increase, decrease, or stay the same—you can't tell from the information given

13. **It is usually considered best to buy stocks in:**
    a) only one industry, such as entertainment or computers
    b) companies with the youngest people on the board of directors
    c) several different industries
    d) only companies that have started in the last five years

14. **The price of a stock may change when there are big changes in:**
    a) the weather
    b) certain laws
    c) styles and fashions
    d) all of the above

15. **The executives of a company are:**
    a) not allowed to buy or sell stock in the company
    b) able to make more money on their stock because they know what is going to happen in the company
    c) not allowed to buy stock in any other company

d) required to announce publicly when they buy or sell stock in that company

16. The easiest way to find out if the stock you bought has gone up or down in value is to:
    a) look in the financial pages in the newspaper or on the Internet
    b) ask your math teacher
    c) call the company
    d) wait until you get the next report from the company in the mail

17. Companies are required to:
    a) invite every shareholder to a meeting every year
    b) tell the shareholders how much they are paying the top executives of the company
    c) report any possible good or bad news that might affect the price of the stock
    d) all of the above

18. A company must send information about how it is doing to:
    a) everyone who owns more than five hundred shares of stock in the company
    b) investment clubs that have at least ten members
    c) teachers that have classes about the stock market
    d) any person or company that owns at least one share of stock

19. When a company shares profit with the people who own its stock, it is called a:
    a) bonus
    b) reward

c) dividend

d) surprise

20. Stock prices can change:
   a) at the three times a day set by the Treasury Department
   b) every time a share of stock is sold
   c) only once each morning, before the business day begins
   d) only once every night, right before the day ends

21. The P/E ratio for a company is:
   a) the percent of executives who take physical education at lunch
   b) the number of computers per employee
   c) the amount of peanut butter eaten in the cafeteria each week
   d) the price of the stock compared to the earnings of the company

22. When you buy an "odd lot" of stock, you are buying:
   a) a number of shares that is not an even hundred
   b) an odd number of shares
   c) shares whose price per share is an odd number
   d) shares in a strange company that does something no other company does

23. When a company goes public it means:
   a) it opens up company headquarters to the public for tours
   b) it issues stock that it sells to the general public
   c) it sends representatives out into the public to take opinion polls about the company
   d) it buys stock in other companies as an investment

24. In 1960, the average annual income per person in the United States was about:

a) $2,000

b) $5,000

c) $10,000

d) $20,000

25. In 2001, the average annual income per person in the United States was about:

a) $10,000

b) $15,000

c) $20,000

d) $30,000

Okay . . . now, grade yourself. Count the number you got right, and rank yourself by the following scale.

25 correct . . . . .Expert: You may want to write your own book.

18–24 correct . . .You're on the money!

11–17 correct . . .You're no Wall Street whiz, but you know the basics.

3–9 correct . . . .You are probably a wonderful person, but money matters aren't your strong suit.

0–2 correct . . . .STOP! Read this book before you do anything else!

Answers

1. A	6. B	11. D	16. A	21. D
2. D	7. C	12. D	17. D	22. A
3. A	8. C	13. C	18. D	23. B
4. D	9. D	14. D	19. C	24. A
5. B	10. D	15. D	20. B	25. D

WHAT IS STOCK, ANYWAY?

Without issuing stock to the public, most of the big companies that produce the things that make our lives easy and enjoyable would not be here today.

Companies issue stock in order to get money to grow into bigger and better companies. Growing companies can develop new or improved products, manufacture more of the things we want, and invent better ways to make things. In addition, growing companies often create more jobs. When more people are working and earning money, there is more money to be spent, and other companies can grow as well. The entire country benefits.

Why would a company need more money to grow? Sometimes a small company suddenly finds that everyone wants to buy its products or services. Imagine a small electronics company that has invented a television that can transmit smells as well as pictures and sound. The owners of the company are sure that as soon as the first Smell-E-Vision TVs are in stores, everyone will want to buy one. How will this small company be able to make enough new TVs to satisfy that many customers?

$WORD
STOCK: a piece, or share, of the ownership in a company

The company will need to buy machines to manufacture more Smell-E-Vision TVs and hire more people to run the machines. They will need to rent a bigger factory space and buy more trucks to deliver the TVs to stores around the country. They will need to hire a lot more people to drive the trucks, to take orders from customers, and to handle the money.

One way a small company can get all this money is to issue bonds. Another way is to issue stock in the company. The people who buy the stock are called shareholders. Each one owns a piece, or share, of the company.

If Smell-E-Vision, Inc., is successful, all the shareholders will share the profits. Of course, there is a chance that customers won't really like to have all those smells in their homes. If it turns out that the idea stinks (ha-ha!) and the company is not successful, there will be no profits. No one will earn any money, and the shareholders may lose some or all the money they invested.

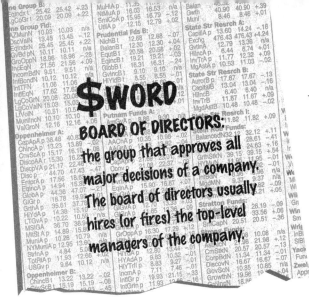

$WORD

BOARD OF DIRECTORS: the group that approves all major decisions of a company. The board of directors usually hires (or fires) the top-level managers of the company.

Because people take a chance when they buy stock and invest money in a company, they usually have the right to vote on some important decisions, like who will be on the board of directors of the company.

Unlike buying bonds, buying stock offers no promise that the company will pay you interest every year, and you may even lose the money you invested. So, why would anyone want to buy stock? Because there is a chance you could make a lot of money if you pick the right stocks!

There are two ways you make money by investing in stock. One way is by receiving a share of the profits the company earns. Another way is by selling your shares of the stock to someone else for a higher price than you paid for those shares.

Why would a company want to issue stock instead of bonds? After all, if Smell-E-Vision, Inc., sells stock and is successful, it has to keep on sharing its profits and letting outside people vote on some decisions. That could really be a pain.

But, on the other hand, by issuing stock, the company does not create a debt. If the company fails, there is no law requiring it to pay back the money it got from the investors.

The executives of Smell-E-Vision, Inc., may not want to issue bonds if they think they will not begin to make money for a long time. They still have to finish inventing the new TVs. Then they have to buy the equipment to manufacture them.

After that, they have to produce thousands and thousands of Smell-E-Vision TVs, advertise them, find stores to sell them, and deliver them to the stores. The Smell-E-Vision executives do not want to have to worry about paying interest on bonds. They also realize that it may be a very long time before they have enough profit to pay back borrowed money. For Smell-E-Vision, Inc., issuing stock makes more sense than issuing bonds.

Let's look at how one imaginary company might use stock to raise the money it needs to get started.

PARTY-TIME PIZZA PALACE

Jennifer, Rachel, Allison, and Matthew all had been friends ever since they could remember. When they graduated from college, they wanted to start a business together. One day, while eating at the only pizza place in town (the one that everyone always complained about), the friends realized that right here, in their town, there was a business opportunity.

They knew that before any business can even begin, the owners have to come up with a plan. They needed to decide:

- $ what would be special about their business
- $ where the business would be located
- $ how much it would cost to start and run their business
- $ where the start-up money would come from

The four friends decided that their

$WORD

CAPITAL: money that is invested in a business to help the business grow

"You know what this town needs..."

restaurant would be in the mall. It would serve great pizza and super desserts, and it would be a fun place to go, with lots of things for kids to do. The next step was to begin to look at what they would need to get started and how much those things would cost.

They would have to pay for:

$ location—deposit and the first month's rent for a space in the mall

$ furnishings and equipment—tables, chairs, plates, silverware, glasses, napkins, dishwasher, pizza ovens, refrigerator, cash register, and computers

- $ utilities—electricity, telephones, and other services
- $ printing—checks, business cards, stationery, envelopes
- $ advertising to get employees—cook, waiters and waitresses, dishwashers, cashier
- $ more advertising to attract customers
- $ salaries for employees
- $ a lawyer to help set up the company and make sure the restaurant met all the local legal requirements
- $ an accountant to set up their bookkeeping and make sure they filed their taxes correctly

They soon realized that there was going to be a lot of money going *out* before any customers or money would be coming *in*. They needed about $20,000 to open their business. The friends had $5,000 to start with. They needed to get another $15,000.

The group did not want to borrow money from relatives. They did not want to issue bonds or borrow money from a bank, either, because they did not want to have the extra expense of paying interest right away. So they decided to issue stock in their business. They looked for investors who would share some of the business risk with them.

The friends, who had named their business Party-Time Pizza Palace, were able to find three investors who would each invest $5,000 in their restaurant. That would give them the additional $15,000 they needed. When they added their own $5,000, they would have enough money to start their restaurant.

Investors in a business can be individuals, companies, or banks. For Party-Time Pizza Palace, there were four investors:

$ Party-Time Enterprises (the four friends themselves)

$ Jennifer's fourth-grade teacher, who always kept in touch with her

$ Matthew's old boss from his summer job at a day camp

$ the local Support Enterprise club

$5,000 $5,000 $5,000 $5,000

In exchange for contributing money, each investor would own a portion of the business, or have equity in it.

Party-Time Pizza Palace issued 10,000 shares of stock. (They could have issued any number they wanted, but 10,000 is a nice, simple number to work with.) Since there were four equal investors, the 10,000 shares were divided into four equal parts. Each group got 2,500 shares. Each share was worth $2.

$20,000 divided by 10,000 shares=$2 per share

Party-Time Pizza Palace opened for business and turned out

2,500 Shares **2,500 Shares** **2,500 Shares** **2,500 Shares**

to be the hottest spot in town. Before they knew it, the friends found that every table was filled every night. They had a terrific take-out business, too. And soon every kid in town wanted to have a birthday party there. After only one year, the friends were able to pay all their bills and still had $14,000 profit to put in the bank!

The friends agreed that they would share some of the profit with their stockholders. They knew that they should not distribute all the profit they had made. They needed to save some of the money to keep the business going. The friends agreed that if the business continued to grow this way, they could afford to make a distribution to the stockholders of $10,000 a year.

Since there were 10,000 shares in the business, each share would earn $1 per year, or 25¢ each quarter (every three months). The money that a company sends to its shareholders each quarter is called a dividend. Every shareholder in Party-Time Pizza Palace would get a dividend of 25¢ every three months for each share owned. So, for 2,500 shares, a shareholder would receive a check for $625 each quarter.

25¢ per share times 2,500 shares = $ 625

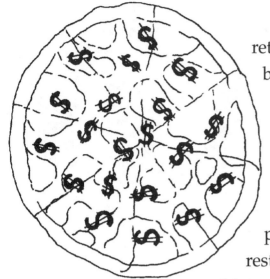

The remainder of the profit, or retained earnings, was kept to help the business grow.

Party-Time Pizza Palace became such a hit that the friends decided to make improvements. They agreed to rent the space next door to enlarge their restaurant. They planned to redecorate the entire restaurant, buy two more pizza ovens, add more tables and chairs, hire more people, put in video games, and add a room for laser tag. They needed a lot of money to do all that—much more than the retained earnings they had in the bank. The friends decided that the best way to raise all the capital they needed was to go public and invite anyone who wanted to buy stock to do so.

Going public is a very complicated process. A special kind of banker, called an investment banker, works with the company to issue the stock. The investment banker helps the owners of the company prepare all the necessary forms and reports. The investment banker also helps the company figure out how much stock they can issue and what the price of each share should be.

The investment banker buys all the stock that the company is issuing. Then, as quickly as possible, the investment banker tries to sell the stock to the general public.

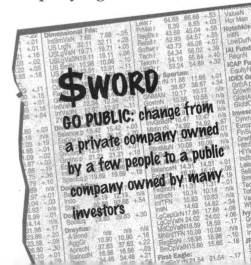

$WORD

GO PUBLIC: change from a private company owned by a few people to a public company owned by many investors

When Party-Time Pizza Palace went public, they needed to raise $500,000. Because the business was so successful, the investment banker advised them to sell the new stock for $10 per share. They would need to sell 50,000 shares to get the money they needed.

50,000 shares times $10=$500,000

The original investors who helped start the company (Jennifer's fourth-grade teacher, Matthew's old boss from his day-camp job, the Support Enterprise Club, and the four friends themselves) were very excited. When the company was started, each investor had bought 2,500 shares for $2 per share. Now that Party-Time Pizza Palace stock was worth $10 a share, each person's original $5,000 investment was now worth $25,000! (Although each investor made a profit, none of that money went back to the company.)

2,500 shares times $10 per share=$25,000

Jennifer's old teacher was so excited that she even bought more Party-Time stock. Party-Time Pizza Palace stock was soon listed in the financial section of the local newspaper. The friends opened new restaurants in malls all over the state. The price of the stock went up to $30 per share, and the dividends went up to 50¢ per share each quarter. And Party-Time Pizza Palace became the biggest success story that town had ever seen!

Almost all the famous companies you know are public companies. There are still a few big companies that are privately held, such as the E & J Gallo Winery, which is still owned by the original Gallo family. Ernest Gallo and his brother Julio started the winery in 1933 with an investment of $5,900. Over the next sixty-five years, Gallo became the largest winery in the world and had sales of over one billion dollars. In 2001, at the age of ninety-one, Ernest Gallo was still the chief executive officer of the company. At that time, Ernest Gallo himself had a net worth of about $800 million!

Levi Strauss started his company in 1853, and in 1873 filed the patent for the first blue jeans. Although Levi Strauss died in 1902, members of the Strauss family continued to control the company. In 1971, the family realized that they needed to make some changes and raise more money in order for the business to grow. Some of the company's shares were traded publicly so in 1985, the family bought back all the public shares and became a privately held company once again.

In 2001, led by chairman Robert Haas (the great-great-grandnephew of the founder), the Levi Strauss company had over seventeen thousand employees and continued to sell Levi's, Dockers, and many other products all over the world. You can learn more about the history of denim, blue jeans, and Levi Strauss at www.levistrauss.com.

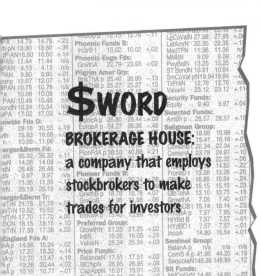

$WORD

BROKERAGE HOUSE: a company that employs stockbrokers to make trades for investors

HOW TO BUY STOCK

In order to buy stock, you must be more than eighteen years old and you must open an account with a stockbroker, who will actually do the buying and selling for you. You can open an account by visiting the office of a stockbroker, by mail, by phone, or over the Internet.

PUBLIC OR PRIVATE?

Can you guess which of these companies
was privately held?

(Hint: There may be more than one in each category.)

Auto rentals:
- ☐ Budget
- ☐ Enterprise
- ☐ Avis
- ☐ Hertz

Food:
- ☐ Borden
- ☐ Hershey's
- ☐ Heinz
- ☐ M&M/Mars

Clothes:
- ☐ Lands' End
- ☐ L.L. Bean
- ☐ J. Crew
- ☐ Tommy Hilfiger

Greeting cards:
- ☐ Gibson
- ☐ Hallmark

Office services:
- ☐ Staples
- ☐ Kinko's

Check your answers below.

THE PRIVATELY HELD COMPANIES ARE:

Auto rentals: Enterprise. Enterprise Rent-A-Car is the largest car rental company in North America. It was started in 1957 by Jack Taylor in the basement of a local Cadillac dealership. By 2001, Enterprise had over half a million cars in its rental fleet, more than 38,000 employees, and over 4,000 locations worldwide. President and Chief Executive Officer Andrew Taylor is the son of founder, Jack Taylor. Get more on Enterprise history at www.enterprise.com.

Food: Borden (which makes "Elsie the Cow" dairy products, Wise potato chips, Elmer's glue, and many other products) is privately held but not by the founding family. The company was publicly traded until 1995, when it was purchased by an investment group. The story of Gail Borden and his inventions and influence on everything from the Civil War to nutrition in America is at www.bordenfamily.com. **Mars** (which also makes Uncle Ben's products, Whiskas and Sheba cat foods, Snickers, M&M's, and other candies). The chief executive officer in 2001 was John F. Mars. His grandparents, Frank and Ethel Mars, started making candy in 1911 and invented the Milky Way candy bar in 1923. His father, Forrest Mars, who took over in 1934, invented M&M's candies. Today, Mars has over 30,000 employees.

Clothes: L.L. Bean. Leon Leonwood Bean began his company in 1912 with the "Maine Hunting Shoe" he invented. Today his company sells over sixteen thousand different items, and is still controlled by his descendents. **J. Crew:** Emily Woods, chairwoman, is the daughter of Arthur Cinader, who started the company in 1983. Ms. Woods owns 15 percent of the company, and the rest is owned by a private investment group.

Greeting cards: Hallmark. Started in 1910 by Joyce C. Hall with two shoe boxes full of picture postcards. (In addition to greeting cards, Hallmark also produces Crayola Crayons and Silly Putty.) Mrs. Hall died in 1982 at the age of ninety-one. In 2001, the chairman was Donald J. Hall, Joyce Hall's son. Two-thirds of the company was still owned by the Hall family and one-third was owned by the employees of Hallmark. More about the history of Hallmark can be found at www.hallmark.com.

Office services: Kinko's. Founded by Paul Orfalea in 1970. Although Mr. Orfalea retired in 2000, he still owns a significant part of the company. Learn more about the history of Kinko's at www.kinkos.com

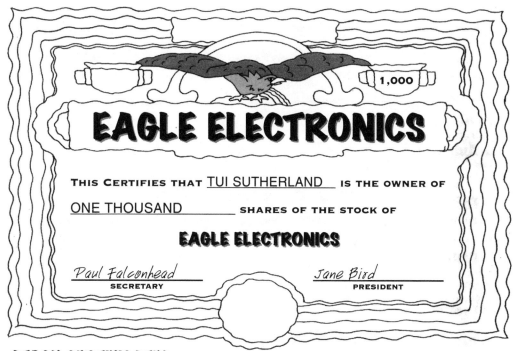

STOCK CERTIFICATES

Until recently, public companies always gave each shareholder a stock certificate showing the number of shares that investor had purchased. The stock certificate proved that you were the owner of that stock, and you had to turn it in when you sold the stock. Now that all areas of investing have become computerized, the information about the stock you buy is usually kept electronically. If you want to have an actual stock certificate, you can still ask for one, but you may have to pay a small extra fee. When stock is privately held, as it was when Party-Time Pizza Palace first started up, the investor receives a stock certificate, but it is not so fancy or interesting to look at. Some stock certificates can be very cool-looking.

NO PROFILES ALLOWED!

If there is a picture of a person on a stock certificate for a stock traded on the New York Stock Exchange, the person must be looking straight ahead or in three-quarter front view.

Chapter Seven

BEHIND THE SCENES

WHO DECIDES THE PRICE OF A STOCK?

The newscasts that report on the stock market often mention specific stocks. They may say, "AT&T is up two points," or "IBM is down three." What does that mean?

First of all, when we talk about stocks, each "point" represents $1. "Up" or "down" refers to a change in the price of the stock. Suppose that at the end of the business day on Tuesday, IBM sold for 115 (which means $115 per share), and at the end of the business day on Wednesday, it sold for 117 ($117 per share). The news reports would say, "IBM closed up two points." If you listen to the news several times a day, you'll hear that the price of a stock can change many times during the day.

Buying stock in a company is different from buying most other things. If you want to buy a book, a coat, or a candy bar, you look at the price tag to see how much it costs. The store or the manufacturer has decided on a price that they think is fair.

You have the choice of whether or not you want to buy the item at that price. If you come back an hour later, it still will be the same price. Even a week later, it probably will be the same price. Sometimes, if you wait long enough, it may go on sale, but no one ever asks your opinion about the price.

Buying shares of stock is a very different situation. Buyers and sellers have equal say in determining what the final price of each share of a stock will be. The price is decided by an auction.

Have you ever seen an auction on TV or in the movies? Maybe you have read a newspaper article about an auction of a famous painting. If so, then you know that anyone at an auction may bid on the item. Each time someone makes a bid, the auctioneer gives everybody else a chance to make a higher bid. When it looks as though no one wants to top the last bid, the auctioneer calls out, "Going, going . . . gone!" and the item is sold to last (and highest) bidder.

Stocks also are sold in an auction, but there are so many stocks, and so many people who own stock, that it would be impossible to auction stocks in exactly the same way as a famous painting.

You often hear

Wall Street

about the stock market. This term refers to the whole business of buying and selling stocks, not to one actual place or market.

News reports talk about Wall Street. In fact, there is a street in New York City called Wall Street, and it's right in the middle of the financial district. In colonial days, there was actually a wall in this part of lower Manhattan, and it marked the northern boundary of the city. Today, the term Wall Street really refers to the entire business of investing. Many people who have jobs in this business say they "work on Wall Street," even though they may never actually go near lower Manhattan.

The actual place where most stocks are bought and sold is called a stock exchange. The biggest stock exchanges are the New York Stock Exchange (NYSE) and the American Stock Exchange (AMEX), both in New York City.

THE ORIGINAL WALL STREET

In 1653, a twelve-foot-high wooden stockade was built to protect the Dutch settlers in Manhattan from attacks by the British and the Native Americans. About thirty-two years later, Wall Street was laid out along the lines of the stockade.

There are more than 140 exchanges world-wide, and they are on every continent except Antarctica. A different kind of stock exchange is the NASDAQ (National Association of Security Dealers Automated Quotations System). NASDAQ stocks are traded over telephone and computer lines, not in a physical place.

Stocks are sold in a two-way auction, where buyers bid on shares of stock and many sellers offer to sell stock at the same

NEWS FLASH FROM THE PAST

The first stock exchange in the United States was established in Philadelphia in 1790.

Investors in Philadelphia soon became worried that the investors in New York would have an unfair advantage. The New Yorkers got important business news first—as soon as the ships from Europe landed there.

Some Philadelphia brokers wanted to fix that problem. There were no telephones then, and even horses took a long time to make the trip.

Finally, they stationed people on high points across New Jersey (which is between New York and Philadelphia) and set up a code of flashes of light that could relay stock prices and other news.

This system worked so well that news could get all the way from New York to Philadelphia in as few as ten minutes!

time. Of course, the people who actually own the stock don't have to go to the stock exchange themselves. There are professionals called brokers who represent the buyers and sellers and carry out their wishes.

In order for shares of a stock to be bought or sold, there must be someone representing a buyer and someone representing a seller. The buyer's broker says how much he is willing to pay for each share of the stock. The seller's broker says how much he wants to receive. If the two brokers cannot agree, there will be no sale. Usually, they reach a compromise and the sale, or trade, is made.

For instance, you want to buy stock in Smell-E-Vision, Inc. You are willing to pay no more than $50 for each share. A person who owns 100 shares of Smell-E-Vision, Inc., wants to sell them for no less than $60 per share. If neither of you changes your mind, the stock will not be sold.

If you really want to buy the

stock, you may be willing to increase your bid to $55. The seller may be willing to reduce his asking price to $55. When the representatives of the buyer and seller agree on a price, they can make a deal and a sale, or trade, can take place.

WHAT MAKES THE PRICE OF STOCK CHANGE?

If many people think a company is going to make a lot of money, they all will want to own a share of that company. Just as in an auction for a famous painting, when many people want to buy the same stock, they keep offering higher bids for each share, and the price of the stock goes up. If a pharmaceutical company announces that it is close to finding a medicine to stop baldness, everyone will want to buy stock in that company.

Sometimes there is bad news that affects a company. Suppose an automobile company has to recall many of its cars because the air bags are not working correctly, and a few months later has to recall other cars because their headlights aren't working properly. People probably won't be trusting or buying that company's cars in the future. People also will not be anxious to buy stock in that company, and the price of each share will go down.

The price of any stock can change many times during a day. Every time someone wants to buy or sell shares of stock, the buyer and seller both must agree to the price before a trade can be made.

$WORDS

BID: the amount a buyer is willing to pay for each share of stock

ASKED: the amount a seller wants to receive for each share of stock

INSIDE THE NEW YORK STOCK EXCHANGE

The New York Stock Exchange began in 1792, when a group of brokers and merchants began to meet under a buttonwood tree on Wall Street. Those brokers set up their own rules for trading and promised that they would always do business with one another rather than with "outsiders."

The New York Stock Exchange is a huge, noisy, busy place. If you are ever in New York City on a weekday, you can visit the stock exchange. It's right on Wall Street, in the financial district. From the Visitors' Gallery of the New York Stock Exchange, you can watch what goes on. (Only people who work at the exchange and some special reporters and guests can actually walk through the trading areas.)

The first home of the New York Stock Exchange (in 1817) was in a rented room at 40 Wall Street. As more companies listed their stock and more people became involved in trading stocks, more and more space was needed. The current exchange building at 18 Broad Street opened in 1903, with one giant trading room. Today, there are so many stocks traded on the New York Stock Exchange (more than three thousand in 2001) and so many people working on the floor of the exchange (over three thousand) that by 2000 the exchange included

$ FACTS

FIRST CORPORATE STOCK LISTED:
Bank of New York, 1792

LONGEST LISTED STOCK:
Con Edison. Listed in 1824 as New York Gas Light Company

WASHINGTON

STOCK EXCHANGE STYLES

People who work on the trading floor wear different-colored jackets to show what their jobs are. Messengers wear light blue jackets with orange shoulder epaulets. Floor traders wear green jackets. Reporters wear navy blue jackets.

69¢

five separate rooms for trading. In fact, the New York Stock Exchange has already made arrangements to build a totally new facility across the street from the current building that will be even bigger!

The central part of each room is known as the trading floor. Around the outer edges of each room are booths. Each of the brokerage houses that do business at the exchange has its "headquarters" in one of the booths. When an order to buy or sell a stock is received, a floor broker from that brokerage house takes the order from his or her booth to the trading post for that stock.

The trading posts are located at the very center of the trading floor. They are the places where the actual buying and selling take place. Every stock is assigned to a specific trading post and is traded only at that post. Each of the trading posts has electronic signs right outside of it. These signs show every stock that is traded at that post, the most recent bid and offer for each stock, and the number of shares that were last traded.

A DAY AT THE NEW YORK STOCK EXCHANGE

At 9:30 A.M., a bell rings to let everyone know that the trading day has begun. The phones start ringing in the booths of the brokerage houses. Orders to buy and sell stock begin to come in from their offices all over the country and all over the world. One of those calls might be from a stockbroker in your town, who is placing your order to buy one hundred shares of Party-Time Pizza Palace stock.

$ FACT

On a typical day, a floor broker walks about twelve miles!

WASHINGTON

As soon as your order comes in, the floor broker takes it to the trading post where Party-Time's stock is traded. He meets a floor broker from another brokerage house who has an order to sell shares of Party-Time Pizza Palace stock. The two brokers try to find a price that is agreeable to both of them. The floor broker buys one hundred shares for you at $12.75 a share.

After the stock is sold, the number of shares and the price per share go into the exchange's electronic system so that they can be reported correctly. The floor broker sends confirmation of the trade back to the stockbroker in your town, who tells you the price the stock was bought for.

Now that you are the owner of Party-Time Pizza Palace stock, you are registered as a shareholder in the company's computer. If you want to get a stock certificate, you can ask your stockbroker to send one to your home. You might want to keep your stock certificate in a safe-deposit box at a savings bank. Or you might even want to frame it and hang it in your room.

71¢

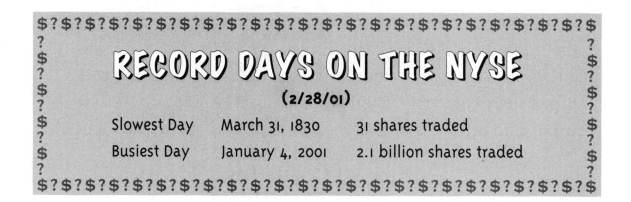

RECORD DAYS ON THE NYSE
(2/28/01)

Slowest Day	March 31, 1830	31 shares traded
Busiest Day	January 4, 2001	2.1 billion shares traded

All day, the floor brokers and the specialists complete trades. At the New York Stock Exchange, there are over eight hundred million shares traded on an average day. (That's almost seven hundred thousand separate trades!) You can imagine how hectic that can be!

Chapter Eight

MAKING MONEY IN THE STOCK MARKET

People invest in the stock market for one basic reason . . . to make money.

There are two ways to make money in the stock market. One way to make money is by receiving dividends, or a share of the company's profits. A second way is to sell the stock to someone else at a higher price per share than what you paid for it.

Before you buy a stock, you can find out how much the company pays each year in dividends for each share. Dividends must be approved by the board of directors. Companies can change the amounts of their dividends whenever they want, but usually they change them only if business has been very good—or very bad.

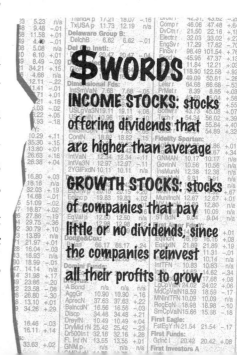

$WORDS

INCOME STOCKS: stocks offering dividends that are higher than average

GROWTH STOCKS: stocks of companies that pay little or no dividends, since the companies reinvest all their profits to grow

People who want to receive regular payments should look at stocks with high dividend rates. Even if the amount of the dividend is not the main reason you are buying shares of a particular stock, you still should pay attention to changes in the dividend rates. Whenever a company declares its dividends, the announcement can affect the price of the stock.

If a company increases its dividend, investors believe that the management of the company has good reason to be optimistic about future profits. More investors will want to buy the stock, and the price will go up. If the company announces a smaller dividend, or says that there will be no dividend that quarter, management appears to be concerned about the company's future and does not want to commit itself to giving out high dividends. This kind of news can make the price of the stock go down.

If you are a risk avoider, you probably will want to invest only a small portion of your money in stocks. When you do buy stocks, you probably will prefer those that pay high dividends. That way you will know in advance how much money you are likely to make from your investment each year. Also, stocks that pay high dividends are usually in well-established companies where there is less risk of losing money.

PRICE APPRECIATION

The other way people can make money in the stock market is to sell the stock when its price goes up, or appreciates. Risk lovers often buy shares of stock in new or small companies. If a new company does become successful, the value of its stock will increase and the investor can sell it for a profit. If not, the investor may lose part or all of his or her investment. Risk lovers accept that because there is also a chance of making a lot if their predictions are correct. This kind of company often does not pay dividends to its shareholders. Instead, these companies keep all their profits to use for their own growth. These companies are betting that they will become very profitable. When that happens, the shareholders will be able to make money because the price of the shares will go way up.

One company that does not pay dividends is Microsoft. People who bought stock in Microsoft when it went public in 1986 have seen huge profits from the increase in price of the stock. If you bought 1 share in 1986, you paid only $21.09 for it. By March of 1999, that 1 share had split into 144 shares (more about that later), and each share was worth as much as $150.125. So, your investment of $21.09 would have grown into $ 13,302 in thirteen years.

Remember, though, that companies like Microsoft are for people who like taking risks. In December of 2000,

$WORDS

BLUE CHIPS: stocks of the largest, most well-established, most consistently profitable companies. It is not an "official" term, and the stocks that are considered "blue chips" may change.

A GAMBLING TRADITION

The term blue chip comes from gambling. In poker, where wooden or plastic chips are often used instead of actual money, the most valuable chips are the blue ones.

Microsoft stock went down to $40.25 per share, making your stock worth only $5,796.00. That's still a nice profit on your original investment of $21.09, but a lot less than you could have had. In fact, it's almost $8,000 less! And that's if you had purchased only one share in 1986! If you had started with one thousand shares, you would still make a profit of almost $6 million, but that would be almost $8 million less than if you sold your shares when Microsoft was at its high point!

Another thing to remember is that strong companies usually recover from downturns in the stock market. By May of 2001, Microsoft stock was back up to $72 a share, so your stock would be worth almost $10,368—almost twice as much as if you had sold it at its low point.

Of course, lots of other companies that do not pay dividends also expect to do very well. Many of these "start-up" companies disappear, along with the money investors paid for shares of stock in them. That's what happened with many of the "dot-com," or Internet, companies in 2000 and 2001. Some companies, like eToys.com and Pets.com, once traded at more than $70 per share. Then they went out of business. People who invested in those stocks ended up with nothing to show for their investment. Other companies, like Yahoo, were able to stay in business, but their shares went from $150 to $18. That means that if you bought stock in Yahoo at its high point, by mid 2001, you would have lost $132 on each share!

MUTUAL FUNDS: THE EASIER WAY

When investors buy stock, they rarely purchase just one single share. Most often they buy several shares in each company in which they are interested. When you look at the prices of stocks, you'll see that having many different ones can be quite expensive. You can see also how much work it would be to keep track of everything that is going on in each of these companies. It's nice to own stock and make money, but do you really want to spend your whole day doing it?

Very rich people can buy many, many different stocks. They can hire people to watch their stocks for them and learn all about the companies and industries they have invested in. That gives them a real advantage in investing.

Suppose you are not one of those very rich people. You still can invest just like they can!

WHAT IS A MUTUAL FUND?

Mutual funds have been around for a long time. When you invest in a mutual fund, you and a lot of other people put money into a collection. The mutual fund manager decides which stocks, bonds, and other investments to purchase with the money from the collection. Everyone who owns a piece of, or share in, the mutual fund gets to share in the profits—or the losses.

By investing in a mutual fund, you can own stocks in more kinds of industries than you could on your own. There are many types of mutual funds. Some invest in only one area (technology, medicine, etc.). Others invest in international companies, or companies that protect the environment. There are mutual funds for kids that invest in companies kids would know and be interested in. There are mutual funds for almost every type of investor you can imagine.

Mutual funds also are listed in the financial pages of the newspapers. You may have heard of some of the companies, like Fidelity, Vanguard, and Dreyfus.

Before you invest in a mutual fund, it is very important to do the same kind of research as you would for an individual stock. Look at how well the fund manager has done in the past. Look at what kinds of companies the fund invests in.

WHAT CAN CAUSE CHANGES IN THE PRICES OF STOCKS?

Here are some things to think about.

$ Laws: If the government passes a law that people cannot buy cars that use a lot of gas and create a lot of pollution, the companies that produce those cars will make less money, and fewer people will want to own their stocks. The prices will go down. Companies that make nonpolluting cars will have better sales and earn more money. The high demand for their stocks will cause the price of each share to go up.

$ Current events: A medicine to cure the common cold would be great for most of us and for the drug company that sells the medicine. Its stock would go up. But what about the companies that make tissues, nasal sprays, and cough drops? People wouldn't need (or buy) their products as much, so the prices of their stocks might go down.

COMMON COLD CURED

In 1995, the Justice Department decided that Microsoft owned too many of the systems that make computers work. It takes a long, long time for the government to make changes in things like this, but by the beginning of 2000 it looked as though Microsoft was going to be forced to split into several smaller companies. Investors got nervous about this and didn't want to buy Microsoft stock. The shares that had sold for $119 in December of 1999 were down to $60 by May of 2000! History shows, though, that investors eventually get less nervous about what the government may or may not do and start to look at the earnings of the company again. That's what happened with Microsoft. The stock started to go back up, because investors thought the company was going to earn money. Unfortunately, it turned out that the company didn't earn as much as they thought it would, and by December of 2000 the stock price was all the way down to $40 a share.

$ Weather: A really bad, snowy winter would be good for the companies that make snowblowers, shovels, snow boots, skis, and snowplows. The prices of their stocks might go up.

$ Government intervention: The government tries to keep everything in business fair and to make sure that there is never a situation where customers do not have a choice of companies to buy from. If there is only one supplier, that company can charge whatever it wants—it's called a monopoly. If more than one company is in the business, competition its created and the consumer saves.

In March of 2000, Cisco (a technology company that makes it possible for Internet users to go from one site to another) was selling for $80 a share. One year later, the price of Cisco stock was down to $19 a share. During the same year, Pfizer (a pharmaceutical company) went from $34 to more than $44 per share!

$ General direction of the stock market: Sometimes, the way investors react to a change in direction in the stock market causes that movement to become even stronger. For a few years, most investors were very excited about technological stocks and Internet companies and their stock prices kept going up. Eventually, investors realized that many of these companies would not earn the high profits they had predicted, or maybe not earn any profits at all. Investors started selling their "tech" stocks and putting their money into less risky, more established companies.

$ Negative publicity: A news article about how some cosmetics companies test their products on animals may result in many people refusing to buy products from those companies. The stocks of those companies would go down.

$ Trends and styles: When many businesses decided that men no longer had to wear suits and ties to work, the companies that manufactured ties began to have lower profits. Other companies that produced sports shirts, sweaters, or casual pants looked forward to much greater sales and profits.

$ Changes in the population: People are living a lot longer than they used to. That means more sales for companies that manufacture things like hearing aids. If people begin to retire at an earlier age, there will be more sales of golf clubs and equipment for other leisure activities.

Investing in the stock market is never a safe bet. You can make a lot of money, but you also can lose a lot of money. Even extreme risk lovers should diversify their portfolios and include some "safer" stocks as well as bonds and other types of investments.

A FABLE

About ninety years ago, when almost no one had a car, people would travel in carriages or buggies pulled by horses. There were many companies who made those buggies and the equipment for them. The company that made the very best equipment was Super Ultimate Buggies (known as SUB).

Back then, there was a fellow named Danny N. Vestor who wanted to invest his money, so he bought one thousand shares of stock in SUB, and paid $20 for each share. He invested a total of $20,000.

Other investors also wanted to own SUB stock. People wanted it so much that a year after Danny bought his stock, buyers were offering to pay $30 for each share! Now Danny's investment of $20,000 was worth $30,000. Danny's mother thought it would be a good time to sell his stock, but Danny wanted to hang on to all his shares.

Unfortunately, Danny did not pay enough attention to the automobiles that had started to appear on the roads. He thought

they were just a passing fad. Danny walked right past the empty buggy-supply stores and hardly gave them a second glance.

Five years later, Danny finally bought his family a car. That same day, he decided to sell his shares of Super Ultimate Buggy and buy stock in a car company instead.

Danny's broker had one small problem when he tried to sell the stock. Everyone else had already seen that there were fewer and fewer horse-drawn buggies on the roads. No one had to be a genius to realize that before long, buggies and buggy equipment would be gone, and SUB would be sunk.

Can you recall how stocks are sold? Remember the auction market, where the buyer and seller have to agree on the same price? Danny was a very willing seller. The problem was that no one wanted to buy his shares of SUB stock. The highest price he could get was $1 per share.

So, Danny didn't listen to his mother. He didn't make $10,000 profit. Instead, this is what happened.

Bought 1,000 shares at $20 each	1,000 x $20 = $20,000 paid
Sold 1,000 shares at $1 each	1,000 x $1 = $1,000 received

$20,000 - $1,000 = $19,000 LOST!

Does this story make you think that it's crazy for anyone to buy stocks? Well, it isn't. In fact, over a long period of time, stocks have made more money than any other type of investment. On average, a person who invested $10 in stocks of small companies in 1926 would have had almost $45,000 in 1996! If that person had invested $10 in stocks from large companies, he would have had almost $14,000 in 1996. During those same seventy years, $10 invested in long-term government bonds would have grown to $337.

Stock prices did not keep increasing steadily throughout those seventy years. During that time, there were some very bad situations for investors. The worst was called the Great Depression. It began in 1929 and lasted through the late 1930s. The Great Depression was a time of terrible poverty all over America, when practically all businesses were struggling. In fact, if you had bought stock just before the stock market crashed in October of 1929, you would have lost 80 percent of the money you had invested.

So, there are two very important words to consider when someone tells you about average increases over a period of time. One word is time; the other is average.

TIME

In seventy years, there have certainly been times when the prices of many stocks dropped a lot, but in general prices have always returned to where they were and then gone even higher. With most strong, well-established companies, if you can ride out the low points and hold on to your shares of stock for a long period of time, you will usually find they will recover from any drop in value and will be worth even more than before the drop.

What if you can't hold on to the stocks for a very long time? What if your college tuition bill is due or you suddenly need to buy a new computer? That's another risk in buying stock. If you need the money at a time when the stock market is at a low point, you can lose a great deal of money.

AVERAGE

Average refers to a group of numbers as a whole, not any one item in the group. You've seen this word often. If your math test scores are 98, 94, 96, 99, and 63 (on the one day you came down with the flu), your average for the year is 90. That doesn't mean that all your scores (or any score) were 90. It doesn't even mean that all your scores were passing.

It is true that, over time, stocks have increased a lot on average. But during that period there have been many stocks that have decreased a lot or even lost all their value. Even in the 1990s when there were so many years of big profits in stocks, there were "blips," or brief downturns, in the stock market.

THE DOW JONES INDUSTRIAL AVERAGE

If you follow the stock market, either on television, in the newspaper, or on line, you often hear about the Dow Jones Industrial Average. The Dow Jones is a daily indication of how well the stock market is doing. The Dow (that's what everyone in the business calls it) is established by taking the average price of thirty industrial blue chip stocks that are trading in the New York Stock Exchange. For example, on April 14, 2000, the Dow suffered its second biggest drop in history! This means the average price of those thirty stocks fell drastically (almost 618 points, or 5½ percent of their total value) and weren't worth as much as they had been the day before. A big drop sometimes makes investors panic and rush to sell their stock. That's what happened in March of 2001. When stock prices started falling, many investors got nervous and tried to sell their stocks. Of course, they couldn't find anyone to bid very high prices for those stocks. In the fifteen days between March 8 and March 23, the Dow dropped 1,520 points and lost 14 percent of its value! When stock prices keep falling that way, we enter what is known as a bear market.

$WORDS

BULL MARKET: a steady increase in stock prices. Even if there is a small decrease, in a short time, prices go up higher than before the drop.

BEAR MARKET: a prolonged period of falling prices, usually 20 percent or more.

SPLITS

Sometimes a company announces a stock split. If the split is "two for one," you will get an additional share for each share you have. The value of each share will be adjusted for the

[stock table fragments - partial newspaper stock listings]

$WORDS

ROUND LOT: the basic unit of sale. For stocks, it is 100 shares.

ODD LOT: a purchase of stocks that is not a round lot (not an even number of hundreds)

split so that you end up having the same amount of money invested in the company. If you had one hundred shares at $30 each, you now have two hundred shares at $15 each. Either way, you still have $300 worth of stock in the company.

It's like a pie. You can cut it into four big pieces or eight smaller pieces. Either way, the whole pie is always the same size. And the amount of pie you have is the same, whether you have one piece of the four-slice pie or two pieces of the eight-slice pie.

Companies may have stock splits for many different reasons. One reason for a stock split is that the price per share might be getting very high. Stocks are almost always sold in round lots (one hundred shares). When the price per share becomes very high, buying round lots is harder for people. A stock split would cut the price per share in half and make round lots more affordable.

In 1965, when McDonald's first went public, their stock sold for about $25.50 per share. You could have bought one hundred shares for about $2,550.

By the end of 2000, that stock was worth about $2,500,000.

86¢

READING THE FINANCIAL PAGES

Do you realize how many products you use every day from companies whose stock you might want to buy? Are you aware that what you, your friends, and your family do every day can have an influence on the profits of those companies and the prices of their stocks?

$WORD

TICKER SYMBOL: a shortened "name" that is different for each stock. Ticker symbols help brokers know they are talking about the correct stock.

Every time you buy something, you are helping that company make money. Let's take a look at some of the things you might do on a typical day. (The letters in parentheses are the ticker symbols/*newspaper abbreviations* for each stock.)

A DAY FULL OF STOCKS

It's 7:00 A.M., and your General Electric (GE/*GenElec*) or Sony (SNE/*SonyCP*) clock radio goes off. You get out of bed and brush your teeth with Crest (PG/*ProctG*) or Colgate (CL/*ColgPal*). As you look through your clothes, you have to decide whether to wear the Tommy Hilfiger (TOM/*Thilfgr*) shirt or the Gap (GPS/*Gap*) sweater. You grab a quick breakfast of Cheerios (GIS/*GnMill*) or Frosted Flakes (K/*Kellogg*). You pick up the phone and use AT&T (T/*AT&T*), Sprint (FON/*Sprint*), or MCI (MCIC/*MCI*) to call your friend for a ride to school.

Your friend's mother drives you to school in her Ford (F/*Ford*) or General Motors (GM/*GnMotr*) car. When you get to school, you head straight to the computer lab, and turn on the IBM (IBM/*IBM*) or Apple (AAPL/*AppleC*) computer.

At lunch, you have a choice of buying Coca-Cola (KO/*CocaCl*) or Pepsi (PEP/*PepsiCo*). Your mother finally picks you up at the end of the day. You stop to do some errands at Kmart (KM/*Kmart*) or Wal-Mart (WMT/*WalMart*), and finish up with a snack at TCBY Yogurt (TBY/*TCBY*) or McDonald's (MCD/*McDnlds*).

LEARNING ABOUT COMPANIES AND THEIR STOCK

There are many places to look for information about different companies. You can learn a lot from the financial or general news sections of newspapers, from TV or radio news reports, from the Internet, from specialized newspapers and magazines, from the company itself, and from reports found in most public libraries.

There are also many places that have information about different stocks, but it's sometimes a little tricky to find the company you want to learn about. In order to find information about a stock on the Internet, or to watch a ticker tape on TV, you need to know the stock's ticker symbol. If you want to look up a stock in the newspaper, you need to know the abbreviation for the stock (which is not always the same as the ticker symbol).

BREAKING THE CODE: HOW TO READ THE FINANCIAL PAGE

To learn about a stock from the tables in the financial section, you need to know how to read those tables.

Stay cool . . . those stock tables are not nearly as confusing as they look. And here's another secret: You don't have to keep this book with you all the time. Most days the newspaper has a little chart that tells you what each symbol means, just in case you forget.

First you need to know which stock exchange lists your stock. For instance, is it traded on the New York Stock Exchange, the NASDAQ national market, or the American Stock Exchange? Once you know that, you look up the company alphabetically by its abbreviation. Here is what a financial listing looks like in a newspaper.

NASDAQ NATIONAL MARKET										
A										
52-Wk High	Low	Stock	Div	Yeild%	P/E	Sales 100's	High	Low	Last	Change
29.25	20.125	ABO	. . .	. . .	19	5	28.875	28.25ᵛ	28.875	+.25
30	10	ADH	.03	10	20	200	26.25	24.5	25	+1
18/8	11.25	AFT	.40	3.3	13	106	12.125	12	12.125	. . .
11.75	6.75	AGX	. . .	. . .	11	90	8.875	8.125	8.875	+.3125
29.25	20.125	ABO	. . .	. . .	19	5	28.875	28.75ᵛ	28.875	+.25

Here are explanations for each of the parts of the stock tables:

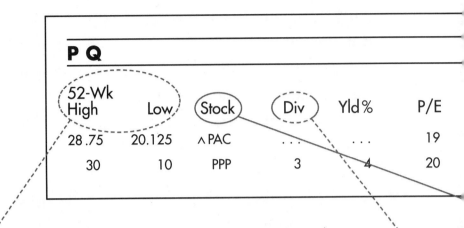

52-Wk High	Low	Stock	Div	Yld%	P/E
28.75	20.125	⋀PAC	...	...	19
30	10	PPP	3	4	20

52-Wk High and Low: Every day, the financial table shows the highest and lowest price for that stock during the past fifty-two weeks. It shows you how volatile the stock is; how much its value has varied in a year. When you look at this section of the stock tables, you can see if the price of the stock today is near the high or low end of its year-long range. Also, if the stock sold for a price that day that was higher than any price in the past fifty-two weeks (or lower than any price in the past fifty-two weeks), a little arrow or dash will appear to the left of the stock name.

Stock prices used to be shown in sixteenths, eighths, quarters, or halves. These fractions represented parts of a dollar. For example: 28 3/4 meant $28.75. All the stock exchanges all over the world changed to decimalization in 2000 and 2001. That's a complicated way of saying that stock prices are now shown in plain old dollars and cents.

Sales 100's	High	Low	Last	Change
5	28.875	28.75	28.875	+.25
200	26.25	24.5	25	+1

Stock: The name of each company is abbreviated by a stock symbol. Party-Time Pizza Palace, for example, might be PPP. Sometimes it's not easy to find a listing for a stock, so we gave you the abbreviations for each of the twenty-one companies in A Day Full of Stocks (see page 88). On the stock table you see that PPP (Party-Time Pizza Palace) sold for as much as $30 a share and for as little as $10 a share in the past fifty-two weeks.

Div: This stands for dividend. Remember, the dividend is the amount of money you can expect to get in a year for each share of stock you own. If the dividend column is left blank with three dots (. . .), that stock does not pay any dividends. Companies that are newer and expect to grow a lot often pay very low dividends or none at all.

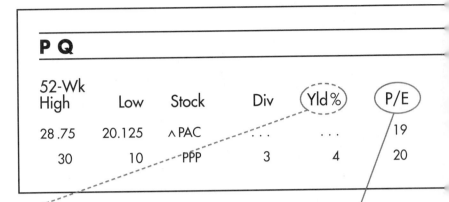

52-Wk High	Low	Stock	Div	Yld%	P/E
28.75	20.125	^PAC	. . .	. . .	19
30	10	PPP	3	4	20

Yld %: This abbreviation stands for yield percentage. It tells you the amount of the dividend as a percentage of the stock's price. Yield percentage is a little like the interest rate for a savings account. If Party-Time Pizza Palace stock closed yesterday at $25 per share, and there is a dividend of $1 per year, the yield percentage would be 4 percent ($1 divided by $25=4 percent).

P/E: The price/earnings ratio (P/E) is another way to evaluate a stock. The P/E is calculated by taking the price of a share and dividing it by the company's earnings per share.

Let's say that last year, a company earned profits of $6 million. All together, the company and investors owned one million shares of stock. So,

Sales 100's	High	Low	Last	Change
5	28.875	28.75	28.875	+.25
200	26.25	24.5	25	+1

the earnings per share was $6.00 ($6 million in earnings divided by one million shares=$6 per share).

Let's also say the stock is selling for $30 a share. So the price/earnings ratio is 5 ($30 price per share divided by $6 earnings per share = 5).

A high P/E number means that investors are willing to pay top dollar for the stock. Why would they want to do that? Because they believe that the company is going to be even more successful and have even higher earnings in the future.

What is a high P/E? There is no set number. Everything is relative. It's important for you to look at the P/E ratios for other companies in the same industry and to see if the P/E ratio for the company you like has changed over the past few years. When the P/E ratio for a stock goes up, it means that investors have more confidence in that company now than they did before.

P Q					
52-Wk High	Low	Stock	Div	Yld%	P/E
28.75	20.125	∧ PAC	. . .	. . .	19
30	10	PPP	3	4	20

The symbol ∧ means that the stock set a record high that day for the past fifty-two weeks, and ∨ means that the stock set a record low that day for the past fifty-two weeks.

Sales 100's: This tells you how many shares of that stock were traded the day before. (To get the actual number, add two zeros to the number.) A "z" before the number indicates the actual number of shares traded, not in hundreds.

Sometimes the volume of trading in a stock is unusually high for a day. Heavy trading often is caused by a news report that mentions the company. If there is good news about the company, a lot of people will suddenly want to buy it, and the price will go up. If there is a bad news report, a lot of investors will want to sell, and the price may go down.

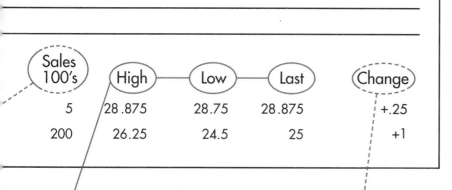

Sales 100's	High	Low	Last	Change
5	28.875	28.75	28.875	+.25
200	26.25	24.5	25	+1

High/Low/Last: the highest, lowest, and last price the stock traded at during that day. These changes are not usually very large, unless there is major news about the company.

Net Change: The net change is the difference between the price of the stock at the end of yesterday's trading and the price of the stock at the end of the day before that. If there is a plus sign, the price went up. A minus sign means that the price went down. In some newspapers, if the price of the stock changes by more than 8 percent, the stock is shown in bold type.

Chapter Ten

BUYING AND SELLING STOCKS

HOW TO BUY AND SELL

Since you have to be eighteen in order to buy or sell stocks, your parents will have to place orders for you until you turn eighteen. They can buy or sell stocks in a few different ways:

Full-service brokers will execute your buy or sell orders. You can visit them in person or talk to them on the phone. They will also give advice on how to reach your investment goals.

Discount brokers may charge less for each trade but don't give you advice about what to buy or sell.

On-line brokers are usually a division of a larger brokerage house. They charge very little for a trade but do not give advice.

$ FACT
DRIPPING ALONG

Many companies have DRIPs (Dividend Reinvestment Plans). When you sign up for a DRIP, your dividends are automatically put toward the purchase of more stock in the company. No brokers or broker fees are involved.

Stockbrokers will often ask you what kinds of buy or sell orders you want to place. The most common are:

Market orders tell your broker to buy or sell the stock at whatever price it's currently trading.

Limit orders let you set the price for buying or selling your stock. For example, if Party-Time Pizza Palace is currently trading at $25 per share and you put in a buy limit order for $20, then your broker will buy the stock for you when it drops to $20. If you put in a sell limit order for $30, then your broker will not sell it until the stock reaches a price of $30.

Stop orders are useful to protect yourself from losing too much money if the stock repeatedly goes down. If you put in a stop order for Party-Time Pizza for $20, your broker will sell the stock for you when and if the price of the stock drops to $20.

THE BULLS AND THE BEARS

In Chapter 8, we learned about how things like laws, current events, weather, publicity, trends and styles, and changes in the population can cause the price of some stocks to change.

Sometimes things like big events in the country or in the world might cause almost all stocks to increase or decease in value. A Presidential election is one of those events. Right before an election, many people may not want to change their investments. They may be waiting to see who will be elected, and how they think that person's ideas will influence the economy. Of course, there will still be some people who want to sell some of their stocks. When there are people who want to sell and not many people who want to buy, the price of stocks may

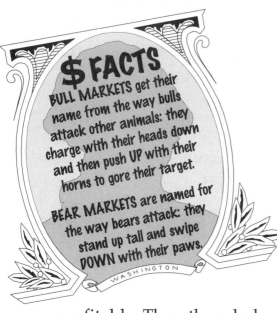

$ FACTS

BULL MARKETS get their name from the way bulls attack other animals: they charge with their heads down and then push UP with their and then push UP with their horns to gore their target.

BEAR MARKETS are named for the way bears attack: they stand up tall and swipe DOWN with their paws.

WASHINGTON

go down. After the election, most Americans tend to be excited about the new president. They think that he will do things to help our country grow. So, investors are willing to pay more for stocks because they think that the companies they are buying stock in will become even more successful and more profitable. Then the whole stock market may go up in value.

During 1999 and 2000, the United States was in a bull market. Almost all stocks were increasing in value. Do you know why that happened? For one thing, many companies were making money, so people wanted to bid more for their stocks. Another reason for the bull market was the increase in value of all the stocks that were involved with the Internet and other technology businesses. Even though most of these companies were not making a profit, people thought that they would all become very profitable, and investors kept making higher bids for those stocks. With so many stocks increasing in value so much, many people became very optimistic about the stock market and kept investing in it. Prices kept going up.

Toward the end of 2000, we began to enter a bear market, and most stocks decreased in value. Why did that happen? One part of the cause was that investors realized that the Internet companies were not going to be as profitable as they once thought. When that happened, those investors wanted to sell those stocks. But who would buy them? Only people who were willing to pay a lower price for them. And what happens when buyers want to pay a lower price? Right! Stock prices go down.

Another cause of the bear market was that investors began to realize that they had bid up the cost of many companies too much during the bull market. When that happens, stocks are described as being "overvalued." Then, as investors start to make more realistic bids for stocks, we say that there is a "market correction," and prices go down.

What should you do in a bear market? Most experts recommend just waiting it out. Over time, the market has always come back up to where it was and increased from there. But no one can predict how long that will take. And remember, if you think you might need your money in the near future, don't invest the majority of it in stocks. You don't want to have to sell your stocks in the middle of a bear market!

WHOSE ADVICE SHOULD YOU TAKE?

There are so many places to look for information about stocks—in magazines, newsletters, newspapers, TV, radio, and the Internet. It's really important to think about what advice you should listen to, and what advice you should really ignore.

No one knows for sure what is going to happen to any stock. Most of the large brokerage firms have people who are experts at analyzing companies and making good guesses at what they think will happen to the stocks of those companies. Those analysts try their best to make good predictions.

There are also some individuals who try to predict what will happen to some companies. These people often post their opinions on Internet bulletin boards or publish them in news-letters that look "official." Every once in a while, there is some-one who does this in an illegal way in order to make money for himself.

How do people trick other investors? Through a trick called "pump and dump." People who manipulate stock (cause the value to change due to their actions) publish lots of things about a company that say how good it is. They might say that the company has a new invention, or has lots of orders for its products, or anything that might make it look as if it's going to be very profitable. Other investors who see these predictions rush to buy the stock, and its price goes up. When the price is pumped up high enough, the manipulators dump, or sell, *their* stock and make a big profit. Because there was not a real reason for the price

THE SEC PROTECTS INVESTORS

The Securities and Exchange Commission (SEC) protects investors in many ways. One of the rules for fair trading is that no one may have an unfair advantage to make more profit than somebody else.

Executives who work for a company usually know more than outside people about whether the company will be very successful (or much less successful). These executives are not allowed to use private information for their own advantage.

of the stock to be so high, the investors who bought the stock from the manipulators have no one to sell it to, and they lose most of or all their money.

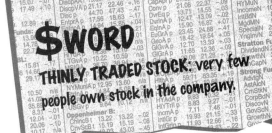

$WORD

THINLY TRADED STOCK: very few people own stock in the company.

It is illegal to manipulate the price of a stock. When manipulators are caught, they have to return any money they made, plus pay a big fine. They may also go to jail. But the worst part is that honest people who believed the manipulators have lost their money and can't get it back.

PROTECT YOURSELF FROM STOCK SCAMS

$ Never act on anyone's advice unless you can verify what he or she says through some other source.

$ Never trust any newsletter that doesn't tell you who is sponsoring it or the names of its authors.

$ Never believe any newsletter if it says it holds stock in any of the companies it recommends.

$ Never invest in small, thinly traded companies, unless you're willing to risk losing all your money.

$ Never invest in something just because someone calls or e-mails you with a great deal or a "sure thing." Remember: If an offer sounds too good to be true, it probably isn't true.

$ Check the SEC Web site www.sec.gov to learn about stock scams and about newsletters and people that the SEC is investigating for doing illegal stock manipulation.

Chapter Eleven

THE GROWING MONEY INVESTMENT GAME

Now for the really fun part—picking your investments and seeing how much money you can make.

You are going to be part of the *Growing Money* Investment Game. You may have played a different investment game in school, and it may have had different rules. The rules for the *Growing Money* Investment Game are in this chapter.

Of course, you will be using imaginary money, so we can afford to give you a lot to work with.

We hereby give each reader of this book 10,000 *Growing Money* dollars.

You are going to pretend to invest this money. You will pick real invest-

SOME SUPER PLAYERS

Several times per year, CNBC holds a stock tournament for kids. One big-winning team was from the 1997 CNBC/MCI Student Stock Tournament contest. They turned an imaginary $10,000 into an imaginary $1 million in three months! This team was an eighth-grade investment club who met regularly with a teacher-advisor.

ments and "buy" them at their real prices. You'll keep a record of the investments you "buy" and "sell," and at the end of six months you'll see how well you did.

You'll find your personal record-keeping pages beginning on page 118. If you and some friends want to see who can make the most profitable investments, just make copies of those pages.

SOME RULES FOR OUR INVESTING GAME

1. Your Goal

You will start with $10,000. The goal is to see how much money you can make at the end of six months. You will play by the actual rules of real-life investing. If you buy a one-year bond, you cannot take that money out to use it for something else. If you buy a six-month Treasury note, you must keep it for six months. You will also keep records of every investment you buy and sell and how much your portfolio is worth each month.

2. Allowable Investments

You may invest in savings banks, bonds, stocks, or mutual funds. Be sure to diversify among different kinds of investments. At least some of your portfolio should be in stocks. You should not own more than four stocks at any time.

3. Interest and Dividends

Mark down the date you begin the game. If you have invested money in a savings account, you get interest at the end of every month. If you begin the game on the fifteenth of the month, you get interest on the fifteenth of every month. To calculate your interest, use one-twelfth of the annual interest rate that the bank is paying. For example: you have $2,000 in a savings account that is paying 5 percent interest; at the end of the first month, you get .417 percent interest, or $8.33.

5 percent divided by 12=.417 percent

.417 percent of $2,000=$8.33

Remember that at the end of the second month, your interest will be 4.17 percent of $2,008.33. With bonds, you get half of the annual interest at the end of six months. For example: you bought a $5,000 bond that pays 6 percent interest. At the end of six months, you would get 3 percent interest, or $150.

6 percent divided by 2=3 percent

3 percent times $5,000=$150

Bonds do not pay compound interest, as savings accounts do. At the end of the second six months, your interest would be 3 percent of $5,000, not 3 percent of $5,150.

If you have stocks that pay dividends, you receive one-quarter of the annual dividend at the end of every three-month period. For example: you bought 500 shares of a stock that pays an annual dividend of $2. Three months after you began the game, you receive dividends of $250.

$2 per year divided by 4=50¢ every three months

50¢ per share times 500 shares=$250

4. Prices to Use

When you buy or sell a stock, use the stock's closing price from the day before to determine the price at which you are buying or selling. You can get this information from the newspaper or the Internet.

5. Stock Selection

When you invest in stocks, consider those companies that make things that you know about and understand.

Now, all you have to do is . . .

That's a famous expression about how to make money in the stock market. It means that when you invest in stocks, you should pick some good companies, buy each stock at a low price, and then sell it at a high price. Sounds easy, doesn't it? Lots of things sound easy . . . until you try to do them. Then you see how complicated each step can be. Investing in the stock market is one of those things. It's easy to learn the basic concepts of wise investing. But then you have to understand more about those concepts, practice what you've learned, and have a little good luck, too.

When you play the *Growing Money* Investing Game, you will have to divide your $10,000 among different types of investments. A moderate risk taker might decide to put $2,000 in a savings bank account, $5,000 in bonds, and $3,000 in a few different stocks. A risk lover might put $2,500 in bonds, $5,000 in two "safe stocks," and $2,500 in one riskier stock.

You've already learned how to make decisions about investing in savings accounts and different types of government or corporate bonds. Since one of the rules of the game is that you must invest some of your money in stocks, it's time to learn how to make decisions about buying and selling stock.

THE BASIC STEPS

The basic steps in investing in stock sound very simple.

$ Pick the categories of stocks that you want to consider.

$ Pick three or four stocks you most want to invest in.

$ Buy shares in those companies when stock prices are low, and sell your shares when the prices are high.

HOW TO BUY STOCK

Step 1: Pick the Kinds of Stock You Want to Look At

Another rule of this game is that you may buy stock only in companies that make products you know about. One reason is that you will naturally pay more attention to those products and the things that affect them, so you will be able to make smarter investment choices.

The first thing you should do is identify some categories of companies. Take a look at the things you use or wear every day. Then think of the brands in those categories. For example, even though your favorite sneakers may be Nikes, if lots of people switch to Adidas, that company will make more profit and the price of its stock will go up. The opposite might happen to Nike. To stay aware of what may influence the price of a stock, be sure to read the newspaper and watch the news on TV. But . . . never forget that *you're the expert*. Even Warren Buffett, the successful investor, agrees that you can learn more and sooner from what you see in your local school, playground, or mall.

It's important to watch and read the financial news, too. By the time a new medicine or invention gets reported in the regular news, investors already know about it. They have bought stock in that company, and the price has already increased.

FAMOUS QUOTES FROM "EXPERTS"

"I think there is a world market for maybe five computers."
—THOMAS WATSON, chairman of IBM (1943)

"640K ought to be enough for everybody."
—BILL GATES, founder of Microsoft (1981).

"There is no reason anyone would want a computer in their home."
—KEN OLSON, president, chairman, founder of Digital Equipment Corp. (1977)

"Who the hell wants to hear actors talk?"
—H. M. WARNER, founder of Warner Brothers (1927)

"Everything that can be invented has been invented."
—CHARLES H. DUELL, commissioner, U.S. Office of Patents (1899)

In 1977, a student named Fred Smith submitted a report for a management class at Yale University. His report was about his idea for reliable overnight delivery service. His professor said that although the idea was interesting, he could not give Smith more than a C, unless the student could prove that the idea was possible to implement. Fred Smith later started the company known as Federal Express.

As far as picking stocks is concerned, here are some categories to start with. We've included some ideas for each, but these ideas are just a beginning. Be sure to add any other companies that you can think of.

CATEGORIES I KNOW

Nike, Adidas, Reebok

Sneakers

Benetton, Gap, Tommy Hilfiger

Clothes

Mattel, Hasbro

Toys

IBM, Apple, Microsoft

Computers and Software

Exxon, Shell, Mobil

Gasoline

Heinz, Kraft, Nabisco, Dole

Food

Toys "R" Us, Staples, Home Depot

Stores

Boston Market, Sizzler, McDonald's

Restaurants

You probably can think of other categories you'd like to add. Remember that we are not making recommendations about the categories or companies mentioned. No one can predict what will happen by the time you read this book. We are only giving you some examples.

WHAT INFLUENCES HOW YOU PICK STOCKS?

Are there some issues that you really care about, like the environment or cancer research? Do you want to help by investing in companies that are working on those issues? Read newspapers, listen to the radio, watch the news on TV. Write down the companies that are doing important medical research or making products out of recycled materials. Or maybe you would like to invest in companies that are in your state or that hire a lot of people from your town. On the flip side, there may be some companies that you may want to avoid. Your parents may have a car that has given them nothing but trouble. It's a real lemon. You may want to keep your money out of that company. What about companies that produce cigarettes, or have polluted a river in your state?

THE STOCKS I WANT TO LOOK AT

Company	Stock Symbol	Exchange	Price	Dividend	P/E

Now that you've picked some companies to consider investing in, the next step is to look at how the company has been doing for the past few years. All of us usually think that winners will keep winning. If you hear about a teacher in the next grade who is supposed to be great, you really hope you will be in her class next year. You expect that she will be great again.

But suppose the Yankees win the next World Series. Lots of Yankee fans will expect them to be winners the year after, too. Sometimes they are; sometimes they aren't. A lot of things can change between seasons. There may be injuries or a change in players. Other teams may get some great new players, or just catch a couple of lucky breaks.

A successful company is a little like a team. With good managers and good products, it is likely to make profits. But if other competing companies start to make the same products—only better or cheaper—or hire the best managers, the original company may start to have troubles. To evaluate a company, you have to look at how it is doing today and also at how it has done over the past few years.

RESEARCH

On the other hand, don't depend totally on the company's history. Successful investor Warren Buffett once said, "If past history was all there was to the game, the list of the richest people would be librarians."

Believe it or not, anyone can get lots of information about any major company. Public companies (companies that sell their stock to anyone who wants to buy it) are not allowed to keep secrets.

The best way to find out the history of the company is to get their annual report. There are three ways to do that: Go to the library, call the company, or look on the Internet.

The annual report will show you the financial history of the company for the past five years. The important things to look at are: Has the company been taking in more money every year (Has revenue increased)? Have there been big changes in expenses in the last five years? What has happened to profit?

Sometimes there is an increase in profit because the company has taken in more revenue. That is a sign of a strong company that is likely to keep growing. Sometimes a company can increase its profits by reducing expenses. Maybe the company closed a factory or bought less expensive materials. If the revenue is not going up also, there is not much chance that the company will grow. No company can keep reducing expenses forever.

The annual report also will explain any major changes that do not result from the regular business of the company. Perhaps the company shows a very low profit this year (or even a loss). That can be bad news or good news. The bad news would be that its products aren't selling very well anymore. The good news would be that the company spent a lot of money to buy another company that will help make them even more profitable in the future. For example, a company that prints newspapers may have a lot of equipment that they use only late at night and in the very

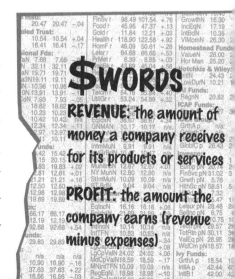

$WORDS

REVENUE: the amount of money a company receives for its products or services

PROFIT: the amount the company earns (revenue minus expenses)

early morning to print the morning papers. If they bought a company that prints catalogs, they could use the same printing equipment in the afternoon for the catalogs. The new, bigger company could make more money than the two small companies put together.

Here are a few reasons:

$ When they were separate companies, they had two sets of equipment, and each was used only part of the time. They can save money by having only one set of equipment.

$ They need only one building and warehouse.

$ They will be buying more paper now, so they may get a cheaper price.

$ They may need only one computer system.

Some other things to look for in the annual report:

$ What does the annual report have to say about the competition? Is there one strong company that has most of the business in this industry, or are there a lot of small companies?

$ What does the company forecast for its growth rate for the next five years?

$ What else does the company do? How big a part of their business are the products you are interested in? You may find that a company that makes cookies also makes cigarettes. Or that film and camera sales are only a tiny piece of a company that makes office copiers and X-ray equipment.

$ Are there any unusual circumstances? Is there any legal action against the company? Does the company have to spend a lot of money to meet new environmental requirements? Public companies must tell you about these things and estimate how much they might cost.

PICK THE STOCKS YOU WANT TO BUY

Now that you've looked at a lot of different stocks, you need to pick the top three or four that you want to buy. Many financial advisors think that these are the most important rules to follow:

$ Look for companies that have been around for a long time and that have had pretty steady growth. A new company with a hot product may be making a lot of money today but may disappear when the current fad is over.

$ Remember that even when you buy stock in a company that looks really safe, there is always some

risk. The American car companies thought they ruled the world, until about 1975. For many, many years, everyone thought those companies were very low risk. Then some Japanese companies (like Honda and Toyota) began to make cars that everyone wanted, and the stocks of some American car companies began to lose value.

$ Use your own common sense. Remember, you're the expert in what you see around you. Look at what people are doing in your school, on TV, in the mall. If Sonic Burgers is always crowded, while Billy's Burgers is usually empty, you have some good clues about whose stock will grow more.

$ Don't put all your eggs in one basket—you should diversify when you buy stocks. That means that your stocks should come from different categories.

If you buy stocks in different kinds of industries, you have less risk. It is not likely that there will be major problems in clothing, automobiles, restaurants, cereals, and airlines all at the same time. By diversifying, you give yourself a safety net. If one investment goes bad, at least your others may do well.

NARROWING THE CHOICES

Go back to your worksheet on page 110. Pick the stocks you most want to invest in. List them here:

1. _____

2. _____

3. _____

4. _____

5. _____

6. _____

7. _____

8. _____

DECIDING WHEN TO SELL A STOCK

The important thing now is to keep track of your investments. You might want to take action if the price of your stock changes. This is the really hard part. Many people think that buying stock is simple compared when knowing when to sell.

If the price of one of your stocks goes down, you may want to sell it so that you don't lose any more money. On the other hand, you may actually want to buy more!

EXAMPLE

EVENT	COST
You buy twenty shares of IBM stock at $80 per share.	$1,600
IBM stock drops to $60. You know that the company is still solid and will rebound. You buy twenty shares at $60.	$1,200

You now own forty shares.
In total, you paid $2,800 ($1,600 + $1,200).

Even though you bought some shares for $80, you will still make a profit if the stock goes back up from $60 to $75, because you bought it at an average price of $70!

WHAT HAPPENS NOW?

To buy stock, bonds, or open a savings or CD account in the game, all you have to do is fill in the Investment Tracking Records. Select whatever investments you want, as long as you follow the rules of the game, and do not spend more than $10,000.

You now own a collection of investments. This collection is

called a portfolio. After all the research and decision making you went through to create this portfolio, it's tempting just to relax and come back in a few years to check it out. Not so fast!

Whatever you invest in, it's important for you to watch your investments to see which you want to stay in and which you want to change. Try to keep a record of the performance of each of your investments. (Remember that gains and losses on stock are only "paper" numbers until you sell.)

INVESTMENT TRACKING RECORDS

MY STOCKS

Date	Stock	Symbol	# Shares	Cost/ Share	Total Cost	Current Price/Share	Current Value	"Gain or Loss"

VALUE OF MY PORTFOLIO

Date	Balance	Investment	Cost (Money Spent)	Money Received	New Balance
3/4/02	$10,000	Savings Account	2,000		8,000
6/4/02	8,000	Interest		6.66	8,006

Once you have completed your portfolio, try to keep a record of your gains and losses for at least six months. You might check on your investments once or twice a week, or, if you get hooked, you might find yourself checking every day. Think about which of your stocks, bonds, and/or funds do well, and try to figure out why that is so. Likewise for the duds. It might be a good idea for you to start a folder for newspaper clippings concerning the companies and industries in which you've invested. That way, not only will you understand why prices are rising or falling, but you'll be able to make informed decisions when it comes time to buying or selling.

Remember, even though investing can sometimes be a gamble, learning the ropes now will help you handle your money wisely in the future. Good luck!

Index

A

American Stock Exchange (AMEX), 66, 89

annual reports, 112-113

average, 84

B

bank statement, 8-9

bank, savings see savings account

bear market, 85, 98-99

bid, 65-68

blue chips, 75, 85

board of directors, 52, 73

bond certificate, 9, 31-32

bonds, 9-10, 20, 30-41, 53, 103, 106

    corporate, 33, 36

    first in the U.S., 35

    how to buy, 40-41

    junk, 39

    municipal, 33, 36

    rating/riskiness of, 39-40

    Treasury, 34

    U.S. Savings, 10-11, 20, 34, 40

broker, 39, 41, 44, 60, 67, 69-72

brokerage house, 60, 96

bull market, 85, 98-99

C

capital, 53, 58

CDs, 21, 28, 117

compound interest, 24-25, 104

coupon payments, 32

coupon rate, 32

D

default, 36-37, 40

diversify, 12, 81, 103, 115-116

dividend, 48, 57, 59, 73-76, 91-92, 96, 104

Dow Jones, 85

E

expire, 32-33

F

face value, 32-35

Federal Deposit Insurance Corporation (FDIC), 23

financial pages, 47, 78, 87-95

G

"go public", 48, 58

Great Depression, 83

Growing Money Investment Game, 102-119

growth stocks, 73

H

I

income stocks, 37

income, average per person, 4, 49

inflation, 3-4, 35-37

interest, 9, 21-29, 31-36, 53, 55, 92, 104

investment banker, 58-59

investor, 7-8, 13-14, 19, 31-33, 36, 52, 55-56, 74-76, 79, 83, 97-98

issue, 33

J

K

L

liquid, 13, 21

loans, 26-28, 31-32, 39

M

maturity date, 32-35

money in ciculation, 6-7

mutual funds, 8, 10, 76-78, 103

N

NASDAQ, 66, 89

net change, 95

New York Stock Exchange (NYSE), 63, 66, 69-70, 72, 85, 89

O

odd lot, 48, 86

P

par, 32

P/E ratio, 48, 92-93

piggy banks, 2-3, 22

portfolio, 12, 81, 103, 118-119

privately held companies, 59-61, 63

profit, 10, 26, 51, 53, 57, 73-77, 112

Q

R

revenue, 112

risk, 10-20, 29, 33, 36-40, 55, 74-75, 80, 84, 106, 115-116

round lot, 86

S

safe deposit box, 24, 71

savings accounts 8-10, 21-29, 104, 106, 117

Securities and Exchange Commission (SEC) 100-101

shareholder, 10, 45-47, 51, 57-63, 71,75

stock certificate, 63, 71

stock exchange, 43, 66-67, 69-72, 89-90
    first, 67
    NYSE, 63, 66, 69-70, 72, 85, 89

stock market, 42-50, 64, 66, 73-86, 98, 105

stockbroker, see broker

stocks, 10
    how to buy, 60, 64-65, 96-99, 107, 114-116
    prices, 64-68, 71, 74-75, 78-79, 89-95
    selling, 10, 52, 65-68, 70-71, 73-74, 96-97, 116-117
    splits, 75, 85-86

T

tech stock, 80

term, 30-33

ticker symbol, 87-89

Treasury bills, bonds, & notes, 34

U

V

volatility, 21, 90

W

Wall Street, 43, 65-66, 69

X

Y

yield, 32, 34, 94
yield percentage, 92

Z

§1.22